FLIGHT PLAN

FLIGHT PLAN

HOW TO ACHIEVE MORE, FASTER THAN YOU EVER DREAMED POSSIBLE

BRIAN TRACY

BERRETT-KOEHLER PUBLISHERS, INC.
San Francisco

Berrett-Koehler Publishers, Inc.
235 Montgomery Street, Suite 650
San Francisco, CA 94104-2916
Tel: (415) 288-0260   Fax: (415) 362-2512   www.bkconnection.com

Ordering Information
Quantity sales. Special discounts are available on quantity purchases by corporations, associations, and others. For details, contact the "Special Sales Department" at the Berrett-Koehler address above.
Individual sales. Berrett-Koehler publications are available through most bookstores. They can also be ordered directly from Berrett-Koehler: Tel: (800) 929-2929; Fax: (802) 864-7626; www.bkconnection.com.
Orders for college textbook/course adoption use. Please contact Berrett-Koehler: Tel: (800) 929-2929; Fax: (802) 864-7626.
Orders by U.S. trade bookstores and wholesalers. Please contact Ingram Publisher Services: Tel: (800) 509-4887; Fax: (800) 838-1149; E-mail: customer.service@ingrampublisherservices.com; or visit www.ingrampublisherservices.com/Ordering for details about electronic ordering.

Berrett-Koehler and the BK logo are registered trademarks of Berrett-Koehler Publishers, Inc.

Printed in the United States of America

Berrett-Koehler books are printed on long-lasting acid-free paper. When it is available, we choose paper that has been manufactured by environmentally responsible processes. These may include using trees grown in sustainable forests, incorporating recycled paper, minimizing chlorine in bleaching, or recycling the energy produced at the paper mill.

Library of Congress Cataloging-in-Publication Data
Tracy, Brian.
  Flight plan : the real secret of success / Brian Tracy. — 1st ed.
    p. cm.
  Includes index.
  ISBN 978-1-57675-497-9 (hardcover : alk. paper)
  1. Success. I. Title.
  BF637.S8T6345 2008
  650.1—dc22   2007043418

Cover design by Richard Adelson.
Copyediting and proofreading by PeopleSpeak.
Book design and composition by Beverly Butterfield, Girl of the West Productions.
Indexing by Rachel Rice.

FIRST EDITION
13 12 11 10 09 08   10 9 8 7 6 5 4 3 2 1

To my wonderful daughter Christina,
a fine young woman, a devoted mother, and
wife to Damon. You are the inspiration
for this book, a wise counselor
and collaborator, and a
role model for all of us.

CONTENTS

The *Real* Secret of Success

A journey of a thousand leagues
begins with a single step.

CONFUCIUS

This is a wonderful time to be alive. It has never been more possible for more people to accomplish more of their goals in all of human history. And if anything, it is only going to get better in the months and years ahead. Your job is to fully participate in what economists are calling "the golden age" of mankind.

In our world, everyone wants to be happy, healthy, thin, and rich—preferably, as quickly and as easily as possible. Throughout history, in response to this almost universal demand for immediate gratification, countless people and organizations have offered enticing formulas, special techniques, esoteric strategies, and secrets for achieving success and happiness without effort.

Every year or two, someone comes along with a book like *The Secret,* suggesting that there is a quick and easy way to be happy and make a lot of money. According to *The Secret,* all you have to do is to think and visualize positive thoughts and you will attract into your life all the good things you want. This idea appeals to people who are unwilling to do the hard work that is necessary to achieve anything worthwhile.

The real secret of success, however, is that there are no secrets. There are only universal principles and timeless truths that have been discovered and rediscovered throughout the ages. Happiness, health, and prosperity do not occur by accident. They are the result of deliberate design and are subject to the iron Law of Cause and Effect.

This law says, "For every cause, there is an effect." It also says, "For every effect, there is a cause or causes." This means that if you do certain things, you get certain results. The Bible says, "Whatsoever you sow, that also shall you reap." Sir Isaac Newton wrote, "For every action, there is an equal and opposite reaction."

Here is a simple rule: If you do what other successful people do, over and over again, nothing can stop you from eventually getting the same results that they do. Conversely, if you don't do what other successful people do, nothing can help you. Success is not an accident. It is not a matter of luck but of design. It is simply a matter of cause and effect.

The Great Discovery

Perhaps the greatest discovery in human history—the foundation principle of religion, philosophy, metaphysics, and psychology—is that thoughts are causes, and conditions are effects. This means that your thoughts create your reality. You do not see the world as it is but rather as you are. Everywhere you look, you see yourself. In a larger sense, your outer world is a mirror of your inner world. Whatever you think on the inside will be reflected back to you on the outside. If you want to know what is going on inside a person, just look at what is happening to him or her on the outside.

This Law of Correspondence—"Your outer world corresponds to your inner world"—is inviolable, at least over time. You can never acquire and hold something on the outside, for the long term, that you have not prepared for and earned on the inside.

You have heard it said that to succeed, you must have what it takes. Well, what it takes is the *mental equivalent* on the inside for what you want to acquire or experience on the outside. For you to change your outer world, you must change your inner world. As Goethe said, "To have more, you must first be more."

In other words, to create a different life, in any area, you must become a different person. You must learn and grow and have the necessary experiences that give you the wisdom and insights to live a wonderful life. And there are no shortcuts.

This brings me to a metaphor for success that I have shared with thousands of people all over the world for many years. When I describe this metaphor, every successful person I have ever spoken to has said, "That is exactly the reason that I am successful today."

Life Is a Journey

Over the years, I have flown back and forth across the country and around the world many times. One day I learned a remarkable fact: when you fly in any airplane headed for any destination, you will be off course 99 percent of the time! Because of unavoidable conditions such as updrafts, downdrafts, crosswinds, turbulence, storms, lightning, and the earth's magnetism, the plane will be off course throughout the journey.

However, when the plane takes off from Los Angeles bound for New York, the pilot will come on the loudspeaker and say something like, "Ladies and Gentlemen, thank you for flying our airline. Our flight today will take approximately five hours and twelve minutes, and we will touch down at LaGuardia Airport at twenty minutes to six in the afternoon. Have a nice flight." And sure enough, five hours and twelve minutes later, the plane lands at LaGuardia, right on the minute, just as predicted.

The point is this: **In life, you will be off course most of the time.** No matter how carefully you plan and organize in advance, your life will be a series of two steps forward and one step back. From the time you start on your journey of life toward your destination, you will have to make continual course corrections. You will have to start, stop, go left or right, move under or over obstacles, and often retrace your steps. These are the essential experiences you require to become the kind of person you need to be to achieve any kind of lasting success.

You Need a Flight Plan

A wise man once told me, "Success is goals; all else is commentary." To achieve greatly, you need clear goals, plans, and schedules to get from wherever you are today to wherever you want to be in the future. You need a flight plan that you *file* before you begin and that you use to guide you on your journey. You must then have the courage to "take off," to step out in faith with no guarantees of success. On your journey, you must be prepared to make continual course corrections. And especially, you must resolve in advance that you will keep going until you reach your destination.

The Real Secret in Action

The most sophisticated guided missile, which will fly unerringly to its target, must first be launched. It must be fired into the air. It must be in motion toward its target before the guidance mechanism can begin functioning.

In the same way, before you can use all your remarkable powers and abilities, you must launch as well. You must take the first step. You must take action. You must overcome your fears of failure and potential disappointment. You must move out of your comfort zone into your "discomfort zone."

The real secret of success is that life is like a long-distance airplane journey. You must first determine where you want to go, board the plane, and then take off toward your goal, knowing in advance that you will be off course 99 percent of the time. And once you begin, you must be prepared to make continual course corrections until you arrive at your destination.

Let the Flight Begin

There are twelve steps you can take on your journey toward greater happiness, health, and prosperity than you have ever enjoyed before. By following these steps, you can take complete control of your life, activate all your mental powers, become the person you want to become, and increase the likelihood that you will reach your destination on schedule. Here they are.

CHAPTER ONE

Choose Your Destination

**Thoroughness characterizes all successful men.
Genius is the art of taking infinite pains.
All great achievement has been characterized
by extreme care, infinite painstaking,
even to the minutest detail.**

ELBERT HUBBARD

Y ou have the ability, right now, to accomplish more in life than you ever imagined possible. You have more talent than you could use in a hundred lifetimes. There have never been more opportunities and innovations to enable you to achieve higher levels of health, happiness, and financial well-being than exist today. In order for you to realize this unlimited potential, your first and greatest responsibility to yourself is to become absolutely clear about what it is that you really want.

When you are absolutely clear about who you are, what you want, and where you want to go, you will accomplish ten times as much as the average person, and much faster as well.

Virtually all of us have four main goals in common. These are (1) to be fit, be healthy, and live a long life; (2) to do work we enjoy and be well paid for it; (3) to be in happy relationships with people we love and respect and who love and respect us in return; and (4) to achieve financial independence so we never have to worry about money again. When you give yourself a score of one to ten in each of these four areas, you will find that most of your problems and concerns today are in that part of your life where you scored the lowest. The most rapid improvements in your life will come when you make improvements in that specific area.

An Abundant Worldview

In flying toward any of these four destinations, you can have either an attitude of abundance or an attitude of scarcity. If you have an attitude of abundance, you will be confident, optimistic, and positive and continually work confidently in the direction of your dreams.

When you have an attitude of abundance, you will tend to see the world in a benevolent way. You will believe that the world is a good place largely filled with good people. You will feel that this is the best of all possible times to be alive.

This doesn't mean that you are unaware of the problems and difficulties in the world. But you accept that these problems have always existed. With an attitude of abundance, you will be more positive and constructive, more focused on solutions than on problems. You will be more concerned about what can be done to improve matters than who is to blame or what has happened in the past.

If you have an attitude of scarcity, you will be just the opposite. You will believe that success is very much a matter of luck and that those who are successful probably earned their money by cheating or swindling someone else. You will see oppression and unfairness everywhere. You will easily accept the old excuses: "The rich get richer and the poor get poorer," "It's not what you know; it's who you know," "You can't fight city hall."

Whichever attitude you develop takes on a force of its own. Your outer world will conform to your inner world. Because you are reading this book, you obviously have an abundant and benevolent worldview. You have a high sense of control and believe that most of what happens to you is self-determined.

If you are a positive and constructive person, you accept a high degree of responsibility for yourself and for everything that happens to you. You do not blame other people or make excuses. If you are not happy with a situation, you get busy and do something to change it. And if you can't change it, you accept it. But you never complain.

Chart Your Destination

The more time you take to decide upon your destination and your goals, the faster and easier it will be for you to reach them. Your future intent will determine your present actions every day.

Begin with perhaps the most important question of all: **What do I really want to do with my life?**

When you set goals for yourself in any part of your life, be perfectly selfish. Idealize. Determine exactly the conditions that would make you the happiest and give you the greatest satisfaction if you could attain them.

Imagine that you could wave a magic wand over your life and make it perfect in every way. What would it look like? What would you dare to dream if you knew you could not fail?

When you ask this question, imagine that you have no *limitations* of any kind. Imagine that you have all the time and all the money, all the knowledge and all the skills, all the friends and all the contacts, and all the education and all the ability that you need to accomplish any goal that you set for yourself. Put another way, imagine that you have a credit card with no limit and you can fly off to any destination.

Your Ideal Career and Income

Begin with your job and career. If your income were ideal, how much would you be earning? If your workplace were perfect, what kind of a company or organization would you work in? What kind of people would you work with? If you could design your job, how would you most enjoy working, and in what ways would you be the most productive? What special talents and abilities do you have that you would like to use at the highest possible level?

Since you are going to have to work at a job for most of your life, one of your chief responsibilities is to be absolutely clear about the perfect job for you. As Napoleon Hill said, "The key to success is to determine what it is that you most enjoy doing, and then find a way to make a good living doing it."

If you could do just one thing all day long and be paid well for doing it, what would it be?

Your Natural Talents and Abilities

Wayne Dyer says that each child comes into the world with secret orders. What are yours? What were you born to do? What are the special talents, abilities, interests, desires, and skills that make you unique—different from all other people? How do you know when you are doing what you are meant to do? How can you tell?

Here are ten indicators that you can use to determine that you are in the right field, doing what you were put on this earth to do:

1. You *love* your job. It interests you, fascinates you, attracts you.

2. You want to be *excellent* at your job, to be among the top 10 percent in your field.

3. You *admire* the top people in your field and want to be like them, to achieve their same level of success.

4. You like to *learn* about your chosen field—to read about it, attend courses and lectures on it, listen to audio programs about it. You never tire of learning more throughout your life.

5. The right job for you is something that is easy to learn and easy to do. It seems to come *naturally* to you, while it is difficult for most others.

6. When you are fully engaged in your work, *time stands still*. You often forget to eat, drink, take breaks, or rest.

7. Success experiences in this field give you your greatest feelings of self-esteem and satisfaction, your *peak experiences* in life. You can hardly wait to achieve success again.

8. You like to *think* about your work and talk about it when you aren't doing it. It is interwoven with your whole life.

9. You like to *associate* with other people in your field and to "talk shop" on every occasion.

10. You plan to do this work *all your life*, to never retire, because you enjoy it so much.

It has been said, "Do what you love; the money will follow." True success comes from discovering what you love to do and then throwing your whole heart into doing it better and better. Determining your ideal job or career is essential to your choosing your real destination and fulfilling your potential.

Your Perfect Personal Life

Wave a magic wand over your family, relationships, and personal life. If your family life were perfect, what would it look like? What kind of lifestyle would you enjoy? Where would you live? What kind of a home would you have? How would you spend your time with the members of your family, day in and day out?

If you are not married, describe the perfect relationship for you. Imagine your dream person. Write down every single quality and characteristic that the perfect person for you would have. You'll be absolutely amazed at how quickly you will meet the right person for you once you are clear about what the right person looks like.

If your personal life were perfect in every way, how would you spend your time and your life? What kind of car would you drive? What kinds of vacations would you take? What sorts of destinations would you want to visit? Create your ideal calendar—day to day, week to week, month to month, and year to year. Knowing what you want is the first step to getting it.

Imagine No Limitations

If your health were perfect, how would it be different from your health today? How much would you weigh? How fit would you be? What kinds of foods would you eat? What kinds of physical exercise would you do each day and each week? Imagine that you could sculpt and shape your perfect body. What would you look like?

Finally, if your financial life were perfect in every way, how much would you be worth? How much money would you have in the bank? How much money would you have invested and working for you? What would be your net worth? How much would you be earning as passive income each month and each year? Especially, what do you want your net worth to be?

The greater clarity you have regarding your answers to these questions, the easier it will be for you to plan your destination and determine your flight plan.

Financial Independence

Here is a simple exercise: Determine how much it would cost you per month to live comfortably even if you had no income at all. Include all your costs of housing, food, travel, medical expenses, vacations, and entertainment. Multiply that number by 12 (the number of months in a year), and then multiply that result by 20 (the number of years you will probably live after you retire). The total represents your retirement goal. This is how much you will have to accumulate to be financially independent for life.

Then determine your net worth. Calculate on paper exactly how much you are worth today. Imagine that you were going to sell everything that you own and move to a foreign country. Be honest. How much would you have in total if you liquidated all of your assets today? This is the kind of analysis that a bank requires when you apply for a loan. A lender wants to know how much you have, how much you owe, and how much liquid cash you have available.

You now have a financial starting point, your current net worth, and a financial destination, the number that you want to reach in the years ahead. You are ready to take action.

Back-from-the-Future Thinking

In determining your ultimate destination in any area of your life, practice "long-time perspective." This technique, used by the most successful people in every area, requires that you project forward several years and determine where you want to be at the end of that period.

You then practice "back-from-the-future" thinking. From the vantage point of the future, in your imagination, you look back to where you are at the present moment. You then think about the steps that you could take, starting today, to get from where you are to where you want to be in the future.

This long-time perspective enables you to see yourself and your life with greater clarity. It reveals what you need to do, and what you need to stop doing, if you truly want to reach your destination.

When you are completely clear about your destination, you'll find it much easier to make decisions regarding your actions, day by day and hour by hour. The secret is simply to make sure that everything you do today, every decision you make, is moving you toward the destination you have chosen.

Four Powerful Techniques

In determining your destination, you can use four special techniques to accelerate your progress and increase the likelihood that you will achieve your goals on schedule. These are *verbalization*, *visualization*, *emotionalization*, and *rationalization*. Let us take them in order:

1. *Verbalization:* With verbalization you write down a clear, specific, and measurable goal. You can't hit a target that you can't see. You cannot achieve a goal that you cannot express clearly in words. The more time you take to be precise and accurate in your description of the goal that you wish to attain, the easier it will be for you to make sure that every step you take is in the right direction.

2. *Visualization:* All improvements in your outer life begin with an improvement in your mental pictures

of yourself and your desired future. You visualize by creating a clear, detailed mental picture of your perfect goal or destination.

Your ability to visualize is one of the most incredible powers that you possess. Each time you replay the picture of your perfect goal as if it were already realized, you imprint this message deeper and deeper into your subconscious mind. The more clearly you can see your goal in your mind, the faster it will appear in your reality.

3. *Emotionalization:* When you emotionalize the goal that you have verbalized and visualized, you actually create within yourself the feelings that you would experience if you had already attained the goal. The more intense your desire to achieve this goal, the more power and energy you will put behind it, and the faster you will move toward it.

When you imagine the feelings of joy, happiness, pride, and pleasure that will accompany the attainment of your goal, you multiply your mental powers for goal attainment.

4. *Rationalization:* You rationalize your goal by writing down all the reasons why you want to reach this goal and all the benefits that you will enjoy when you attain it. Make a list of all the ways that the attainment of this goal will improve your life. As Nietzsche wrote, "He who has a strong enough why can bear almost any how."

Reasons are the fuel in the furnace of achievement. The more reasons you have for wanting to attain a goal, the more motivated and determined you will become. The more reasons you have, the more you will persist in the face of any adversity. The more reasons you have, the more creative you will become in overcoming difficulties and removing obstacles. The more reasons you have, the more likely it is that you will become *unstoppable* in your movement toward your destination.

Make It Believable

One important point: make sure your goals are both believable and realistic. As Napoleon Hill said, "Whatever the mind of man can conceive and believe, it can achieve."

When you decide on an exciting future destination, your goal must be realistic. It must be something that you can get your mind around. It must be something that makes you stretch but that you feel confident you can achieve.

This is the reason for making your goals believable: if you set a goal that is too far beyond anything you have ever accomplished, it actually *demotivates* you rather than motivating you. When you set your goals too high, a "circuit-breaker" mechanism in your subconscious mind actually shuts off your motivation.

If you cannot quite believe in your *conscious mind* that you can attain a goal, none of your mental powers will click into action to help you attain it. Instead, you may be motivated and excited for a while, but as soon as you face the inevitable adversity and disappointment that accompany goal attainment, you will lose heart and give up.

Walk Before You Run

Quite often, people will come up to me after a seminar and say that they have decided upon their financial goal. When I ask them what it is, they tell me that they have decided to become a millionaire or even a billionaire in the next year or two.

In almost every case, these people turn out to have no money or very little. They are often in their thirties or forties and have a lifetime of financial mismanagement behind them. Nonetheless, they think that they can neutralize all their past experiences and somehow leap into wealth and affluence with little preparation, few resources, and no clear idea of how to get there. They believe that all they need to do is to think happy thoughts and they will magically attract everything they need to overcome decades of frustration and failure.

When people say to me that they want to be a millionaire as soon as possible, I suggest that they first become a "thousandaire." After they have managed to save a thousand dollars and get out of debt, they can then become a "ten thousandaire," and so on. To achieve great things,

great efforts are necessary. Each person must walk before
he or she can run.

The Question of Deservingness

The great frontier today is not outer space. Rather, it is
inner space—recognizing and releasing the incredible
powers of the mind.

Because of childhood experiences and other factors,
you have deep within you a series of psychological
blocks—"mental brakes" on your potential. One of the
first steps to achieving great things is for you to identify
and release these mental brakes so that you can move
ahead in your life far faster than ever before.

One of the most harmful of these unconscious barriers
is the feeling of undeservingness. This occurs when you
feel, deep in your heart, that you do not really deserve to
be happy, healthy, and prosperous. Most people have this
feeling of undeservingness to some extent, and for many
people, it becomes a major obstacle to their success. This
block is expressed in the feeling "I'm not good enough."

Create Value for Others

The fact is that you deserve all the good things in life that
you can possibly imagine as long as you achieve them by
doing or contributing something of value to other people
and to your world. When you develop your talents and

skills, work hard, and do good work that benefits other people, you deserve all the recognition and rewards that you earn. You do not need to feel guilty or undeserving in any way. When you contribute value to the lives of others, you are entitled to keep some of that value for yourself. This simple concept is the basis of free markets and free societies.

When you achieve great financial success, people may ask you, "Don't you feel guilty making all that money?" You can reply with pride and confidence, "Not at all. I have decided that the very best way to help the poor is not to become one of them."

The Practice of Voluntary Exchange

This brings us to an important point. All money comes from creating wealth of some kind. Most money that a person possesses is the result of that person exchanging his or her time and effort in the production of a product or service for a particular amount of money.

In other words, every dollar that you desire to acquire on your road to financial independence has to come from someone who has worked to earn the money in some way. Every dollar that you wish to acquire must be given to you or paid to you voluntarily by someone else who has worked hard to earn that amount of money for himself or herself.

The key question in life then becomes, What can I do to *deserve* this money from other people?

The Power of Contribution

Peter Drucker said that most of our misunderstandings in business and finance could be eliminated if we just replaced the word "success" with the word "contribution."

When you look around, you will find that the wealthiest people are those who are making the greatest contributions to the greatest number of people. They are producing products and services that large numbers of people are willingly and eagerly buying to improve the quality of their own lives.

The question you must ask and answer is, What contribution am I going to make to other people to cause them to want to give me the amount of money I want to earn or acquire? This may be the most important question of all with regard to your financial life. What are you doing today? What can you do in the future? Why do you deserve the kind of money that you want to acquire? What value are you prepared to give to others so that they will voluntarily give you their money, the money that they have earned from their personal efforts?

Most of all, what kind of a person do you have to become on the inside, in terms of knowledge, skills, and character, to deserve the kind of life you want to live on the outside?

When you stop thinking about yourself and what you can get and start projecting into the minds and hearts of the people you wish to serve, you will see all kinds of possibilities and opportunities to help others. When you begin focusing on giving, you will truly step onto the road to riches.

CHAPTER TWO

Review Your Flight Options

**Our grand business is not to see
what lies dimly in the distance,
but to do what lies clearly at hand.**

THOMAS CARLYLE

O nce you have become clear about who you are, what you want, and what your true goals are in each area of your life, you can begin to evaluate all the different routes by which you can reach your destination. Now you can determine the strategies and tactics that you can use to achieve your goals and arrive at your destination on schedule.

Develop Options Continually

One of the most important rules that I have ever learned is this: You are only as free as your well-developed options.

For example, if you have only one way to accomplish a task and that method does not work, you will be stopped in your tracks. If you have only one option or alternative to achieve a goal or to reach a destination and that one way fails for any reason, you can find yourself stranded.

Successful people are continually developing options, just in case something doesn't work out the way they had intended. They develop alternate courses of action to insure against unexpected setbacks or reversals. As a result, when things go wrong, as they always do, successful people remain calm and relaxed. They have already thought through the worst possible situations that could occur and have a plan ready-made to deal with them.

Increase Your Options

If your goal is to achieve a superb level of physical fitness, make a list of seven actions that you could take today to start becoming fit, trim, and healthy. What should you start doing or stop doing? How should you plan each day, from the time you wake up in the morning, if you want to achieve superb levels of health and fitness?

If your goal is to have a happy family or to find a wonderful relationship, make a list of everything that you could do to make your wishes come true. Ask the important people in your life what you could do more of or less of to improve your relationships with them. What would they like you to start doing or stop doing to make them happier?

Good Choices and Better Decisions

All of life is a series of choices and decisions. The quality of your life today has been largely determined by the quality of the choices and decisions that you made in the past. The quality of your life in the future will be determined by the choices and decisions that you make today, especially in those areas that are critical for achieving your goals and reaching your destination.

Your choice of a particular job or particular company to work for or business to start can change the entire direction of your life and destiny. You must therefore take enough time to think through and be completely comfortable with your choice before you make a final decision.

One of the concepts that we teach in our advanced coaching programs is the idea of "hourly rate." We have all of our clients divide their annual income by 2,000, the approximate number of hours that an executive or entrepreneur works in a year. This amount is their hourly rate.

For example, if you earn $50,000 a year and you divide that amount by 2,000, you come up with a rate of $25 per hour. If you earn $100,000 per year, your hourly rate is $50.

Before you can plan your time and your life, you must be absolutely clear about both the hourly rate that you are earning today and the hourly rate that you want to earn in the future. Every hour that you spend on a low-value or no-value activity is costing you $25, $50, or more. Everything that you choose to do in the course of your working day is either earning or costing you money at your desired hourly rate.

Determine the Highest and Best Use of Your Time

Whatever job you choose to take, company you choose to work with, investment you choose to make with your money, or time you choose to spend on a particular activity, think it through carefully in advance and be certain that you are making the highest and best use of your time and resources.

If you are not happy with your current "seat selection," be proactive rather than passive. If you are not happy with your current job, get busy and find something better. If you're not happy with your current relationship, improve it if you can, and be prepared to walk away if you can't.

Refuse to Settle

Abraham Maslow once wrote, "The story of the human race is the story of men and women selling themselves short."

Many people, because of fear and timidity, settle for far less than they are truly capable of achieving. They stay in jobs they don't like. They stay in relationships that don't make them happy. They engage in health habits that are harmful to them. They invest their money in things they don't understand and leave the money there long after they realize they've make a mistake.

If you are not satisfied with any part of your life, with your current seat selection, remember that you can always pay a price to be free. And you will always know what that price is.

Ask for What You Want

In business and in your personal life, remember that every term or condition that you are ever offered has been decided by someone and can be changed by someone else. Whether this involves the pay and conditions of a job, the terms of a contract, the costs of products or services, rental or lease rates of offices or equipment, or bank terms for loans or lines of credit, if you are not happy for any reason, don't be reluctant to ask for something different.

Remember that *before* you ask, the answer is always no. If after you ask, the answer is still no, then all you have lost is a few seconds of your life. But if the answer is yes, it can change your entire future.

You know the old saying, "Nothing ventured, nothing gained." And the Bible says, "You have not because you ask not." Never be afraid to ask.

Cast a Wide Net

The rule with ideas is this: Quality is a function of quantity. This means that the more ways to achieve your goal that you consider before you embark on your journey, the better will be the quality of the choice you make.

Cast a wide net. Don't fall in love with the first idea that occurs to you. You must continually remind yourself that *emotions distort evaluations*. This means that the more emotional you become about a course of action at the beginning, the less able you will be to make the best decisions and determine the best way for you to reach your destination.

Become Your Own Consultant

Imagine that you are a consultant who has been brought in to advise yourself on the very best course of action for you to take to achieve a goal or reach a destination. As your own consultant, force yourself to remain calm, cool, and objective about the advice that you give to yourself.

There is a definite time for emotion, passion, enthusiasm, and commitment in a decision. But it is only *after* you have decided on the very best way for you. Up to that time, you should remain as detached and as objective as possible to ensure that you make the right decision.

Don't fall in love with your ideas, especially your initial ideas. Always be open to the possibility that there is a better way to achieve the same goal.

The Foundation of Riches

If your goal is financial success, there is only one way to attain it permanently and that is to "add value." All long-term, predictable, and enduring wealth comes from adding value in some way. It comes from serving other people by providing them with products and services that they want and need and are willing to pay for, in competition with others who also want to sell these people similar or different products and services. This is a basic economic principle, and it is inviolable in the long term.

Perhaps the greatest law of the Bible is the Law of Sowing and Reaping. "Whatsoever you sow, that also shall you reap." Whatever you sow in your career, family, health, and financial life is what you will reap in your experience. Whatever you are reaping today is the direct result of what you have sown in the past. If you are not happy with your current "crop," begin today to sow something different. Begin today to add value to others in a superior fashion.

Notice also that this is not the "Law of Reaping and Sowing." Always, the sowing comes first and often goes on for a long time before you reap the harvest.

According to Thomas Stanley and William Danko in their book, *The Millionaire Next Door*, the average self-made millionaire in America has invested twenty-two years of hard work, sacrifice, reversals, difficulties, and temporary failures to reach that amount of wealth. People who think that they are going to beat the averages and jump to the front of the financial line are usually unprepared to put in the hard work necessary, and as a result, they end up at the back of the line all their lives. Don't let this happen to you.

Start with a List

If your goal is financial, make a list of as many different ways as possible to achieve the same financial results. The more choices you have, the better decision you will make. Here are eight examples:

1. You could achieve your goal by starting a new business.

2. You could buy an existing business and make it more profitable.

3. You could become excellent at what you do, become very well paid for doing it, and carefully invest and save your money over the course of your career.

4. You could invest in real estate of some kind, either to renovate and resell or to rent out and manage.

5. You could contribute your special talents and skills to a start-up business in exchange for stock options if the company is successful.

6. You could buy a franchise and make it successful.

7. You could turn your hobby or area of interest into a moneymaking opportunity.

8. You could dedicate yourself to working for a successful company, become absolutely excellent in your
work, and become one of the highest paid people
in your field. With these high earnings, properly
invested, you could become wealthy.

Each one of these methods has been tried and proven
by millions of people who started with nothing and became millionaires. And every one of them requires that
you become very good at serving others in some way.

Hope Is Not a Strategy

Remember, *hope is not a strategy*. Investigate before you
invest your time, money, or emotion in a job, business, or
relationship. Examine every detail of the proposed route
to your destination.

Get advice from others who have traveled the same
route. Learn from the experts. Ask people who have
reached the same destination how they did it and what
they learned. Ask them what they would do differently
if they had to take this trip over again.

In reviewing your options, always be open to the possibility that you could be completely wrong. Be willing to
admit it, and take a different route if necessary.

It has been said that the shortest distance between
two points is a straight line. This may or may not be true
when it comes to moving from where you are to your

goals. Sometimes, a roundabout method is actually a faster way to get there.

Many people today are realizing that the achievement of their financial goals requires that they upgrade their education and skills. They are enrolling in community colleges, seeking online degrees, attending courses and seminars, and reading voraciously in their fields. They are cultivating and fertilizing the soil so that they can ultimately reap a greater crop.

Your Ability to Think

The most valuable asset you have in achieving your goals and reaching your destination in life is your mind. The value is contained in your ability to think clearly about who you are and what you want. Fully 80 percent or more of all your success will come as the result of your having taken the time to think clearly and accurately, in advance, about exactly what you want to accomplish in life and what success will look like.

Your ability to set clear, specific, measurable goals that you intensely desire and that are in harmony with your very best talents and abilities is the first real step to reaching your destination and to lifelong success.

CHAPTER THREE

Write Your Flight Plan

Our goals can only be reached through the vehicle of a plan, in which we must fervently believe, and upon which we must vigorously act. There is no other route to success.

STEPHEN A. BRENNEN

Many people think that having a clear goal and being positive and optimistic about accomplishing it is all they need to do to be happy and successful. However, choosing your destination, although vitally important, is just the starting point. Now the real work begins. Now is when you demonstrate to yourself and to others that you are really serious about your goal.

The fact is that only 3 percent of people have clear, written goals with plans to accomplish them. Only about 3 percent of adults work on their most important goals each day. Only the top people think about their goals most of the time.

Instead of goals, the great majority have *wishes*. They have hopes, dreams, and fantasies. They have what I call "cigarette smoke" goals. They dissipate quickly and fade away in the imagination, providing no clarity of focus and direction.

Your dream house, your dream business, your dream relationship, or your dream job remains just that, a dream, until you put some "meat on the bones." Only when you thoroughly plan and prepare every detail of your journey can you be assured of reaching your destination on schedule.

You Need Both a Measure and a Method

Define your goals both qualitatively and quantitatively. When you define a goal *qualitatively*, you determine how you will think and feel as the result of having achieved that goal. You imagine the feelings of pride, satisfaction, joy, happiness, love, peace, and pleasure that you would have if you achieved the perfect goal for you, as you have defined it. You create those feelings within yourself by imagining that you have already achieved your goal.

You define a goal *quantitatively* by attaching specific numbers to it. This gives you a target to aim at and allows you to track your progress. If you can't measure it, you can't manage it.

For example, all people say that they want to be financially independent. But when you ask them what that means, the best they can usually come up with is "I want to be a millionaire."

But this goal is too vague. "Financial independence" means that you have enough money so that you never have to worry about money again. So the question is, What is your number? How much will you actually need?

Goal Setting Made Simple

Before you actually "take off" toward your destination, you can take a series of planning steps to dramatically increase the probability that your trip will be successful.

1. Decide exactly what you want in each area of your life. Be specific. Define your goal so clearly that a child could understand it and explain it clearly to another child.

   For example, instead of saying, "I want to make a lot of money," you must be clear about exactly how much "a lot" means. You can't become motivated and determined to accomplish something that is unclear or fuzzy.

2. Write down your goal and make it measurable. A goal that is not in writing is merely a wish, "a goal with no energy behind it." When you make it measurable, you create a clear target to aim at.

3. Set a deadline. Be absolutely clear about when you want to achieve this goal. Your subconscious mind loves deadlines. They activate your mental powers and drive you forward.

4. Identify all the obstacles that you will have to overcome to achieve your goal. What could possibly go wrong? What stands between you and your goal? Why aren't you at your goal already? What is holding you back or could hold you back?

   Think on paper! The more clearly you identify all the various problems and difficulties you could experience, the better prepared you will be to solve or remove them, should they occur.

5. Determine the additional knowledge and skills that you will require to achieve your goal. Remember, to accomplish something that you have never achieved before, you will have to learn and practice something that you have never done before. Whatever got you to where you are today is not enough to get you any further. Every new goal requires the acquisition and application of a new piece of knowledge or a new skill. What is it for you? Clarity is essential.

6. Determine those people whose help and cooperation you will require to achieve your goal. To accomplish large goals, you will need the help of many people. The greater clarity you have about who those people actually are, the more likely it is that you will take

the steps necessary to earn their cooperation and support.

7. Make a list of all your answers to the above and organize them by sequence and priority. What do you need to do first? What is most important? A list of activities organized by sequence and priority is a *plan*, a step-by-step series of tasks that lead you inevitably toward your goal, your destination.

By following these seven steps, you can accomplish almost any goal that you set for yourself. Following is a simple formula that you can use to determine your most important destination, your number one goal.

The Guaranteed Success Formula

With this formula, you can transform your life and reach your most important destination on schedule. It consists of four simple steps. People all over the world have told me that these four steps have enabled them to accomplish more faster than they ever dreamed possible.

Step One: Use the Ten-Goal Method

Take a clean sheet of paper and write the word "Goals" and today's date at the top. Write down ten goals that you would like to accomplish sometime in the future. Use the "magic wand" technique and imagine that you have no

limitations of any kind. Write down ten things that you
would like to be, have, or do in the future as if each one of
them were guaranteed to happen:
Here are a few guidelines:

1. Write in the *present* tense, as though your goal had
   already been achieved. Instead of writing, "I *will*
   earn $XXX each year," write, "I earn $XXX each year."
   Your subconscious mind can register commands
   that are phrased in the present tense only.

2. Write in the *positive* tense. Instead of writing,
   "I will quit smoking" (negative), you would write,
   "I am a nonsmoker" (positive).

3. Write in the *personal* tense. For this exercise, and
   for the rest of your life, begin each goal with the
   word "I." You are the only person in the universe
   who can use the word "I" with reference to yourself.
   When you begin a positive affirmation for a goal
   with the word "I," it is immediately accepted by
   your subconscious mind and your superconscious
   mind as an important command coming down
   from the "head office."

Each of your ten goals should begin with the word "I";
be in the present, positive, personal tense; and end with
the deadline words "by _____ ."

Step Two: Select Your Most Important Goal

Once you have written out your goals, imagine that you will achieve all of them, sooner or later, if you want them long enough and hard enough. But also imagine that you could choose any one of these goals and have it come true within twenty-four hours.

Now ask yourself this question: **What one goal on this list, if I could achieve it right now, would have the greatest positive impact on my life?** Whatever your answer to that question, circle that goal. This now becomes your major *definite purpose*, your primary goal, and your most important destination for the next leg of your life's journey.

Step Three: Make a Plan

Transfer this goal to the top of a clean sheet of paper. Be sure to write it in the present, positive, personal tense—describing it exactly as if you had already attained it—and set a deadline for completion.

Make a list of the difficulties you will have to overcome, the additional information and skills you will require, and the people whose cooperation you will need to achieve this goal. Organize this information into a plan, and then take action immediately to begin moving toward your destination.

Step Four: Practice Mindstorming on Your Goal

Mindstorming forces you to concentrate intensely on how to achieve your goal. Take a new sheet of paper and write your major definite purpose at the top of the page in the form of a question. For example, if your goal was financial, you could write, "How can I earn $XX,XXX by December 31, 2____?"

Then discipline yourself to write *twenty* answers to this question. You can write more than twenty answers, but you must write a minimum of twenty responses to your question.

Your first three to five answers will be fairly simple. You will write that you could do more of this or less of that. The next five answers will be more difficult and will require greater creativity. The last ten answers will require incredible concentration and discipline. You will have to dig deep into the resources of your creative mind to reach your goal of twenty answers.

Take Action

Once you have generated twenty answers, select one of those answers and take action on it immediately. This is very important. When you take action on one of these ideas, you will unlock your inborn reserves of creativity. All day long, you will have new ideas to solve your problems and achieve your goals. You will start to perform at exceptional levels.

If you do not immediately do something with at least one of these ideas, the flow of creativity will slow down and stop. You will get little benefit. Nothing will happen.

There is a direct relationship between how quickly you take action on a new idea and how likely it is that you will ever take action on any new ideas in the future.

When you develop the habit of intense action orientation, you will step on the accelerator of your own potential. You will begin moving rapidly toward the achievement of your most important goal.

Conduct this exercise regularly throughout your life. Whenever you are going through a period of transition or need to plan a new destination, make a list of ten goals, select the most important one, and discipline yourself to generate twenty ways to accomplish it. Then select one idea and take action on it immediately.

Back from the Future Again

Project forward in your mind to your deadline for achieving your goal. Imagine that everything has worked out perfectly and that you have reached your destination exactly as you planned and on the schedule you set for it.

Looking back from the perspective of success, from the future, to where you are today, complete this sentence with at least twenty answers: "I achieved this goal because I . . ." Write down everything that you can think of that you could have done to ensure that you were successful.

Next, take another sheet of paper and complete this sentence: "I failed to achieve my goal because I didn't . . ." Make a list of everything that you could have done but didn't do that caused you to fail to reach your destination.

This combination of exercises forces you to think with greater clarity than most people have in their lifetimes. By completing these sentences with ten or twenty answers, you will immediately see things you should do or should not do to ensure your success.

Create a positive affirmation for your number one goal: "My major definite purpose is to earn $XX,XXX by December 31, 2____ ." You then create a clear mental picture of how your life would be different when you achieve your goal. You imagine how you will feel when you achieve your goal. You think of all the reasons why you want this goal in the first place.

Finally, you resolve to do something every day, without exception, until your goal is achieved. You get going and you keep going. Remind yourself, with regard to your most important goal, that failure is not an option!

EXERCISE
Writing Your Flight Plan

Make a list of **ten goals** you would like to achieve in the next year:

1. _____

2. _____

3. _____

4. _____

5. _____

6. _____

7. _____

8. _____

9. _____

10. _____

What **one goal** on this list would have the greatest positive impact on your life if you were to accomplish it within twenty-four hours?

_____

_____

_____

What is your **deadline** for achieving this goal?

_____

_____

List three **problems** or **obstacles** that stand in your way of achieving this goal:

1. _____

_____

2. _____

_____

3. _____

_____

List three additional **skills** or **forms of knowledge** that you will require to achieve this goal:

1. _____

2. _____

3. _____

List the three most important **people, groups, or organizations** whose help and cooperation you will require to achieve this goal:

1. _____

2. _____

3. _____

Based on your answers to the above, make a list of **seven steps** you could take immediately to begin achieving this goal:

1. _____

_____

2. _____

_____

3. _____

_____

4. _____

_____

5. _____

_____

6. _____

_____

7. _____

_____

What **one action** are you going to take immediately to begin moving toward your destination?

_____

_____

Whatever your answer to the last question, launch immediately. Don't wait. Move fast. Take off on your journey, and don't look back.

CHAPTER FOUR

Prepare for Your Journey

Are you in earnest? Seize this very minute!
Boldness has power, and magic in it.
Only engage, and the mind grows heated.
Begin it, and the work will be completed.

JOHANN WOLFGANG VON GOETHE

Preparation is the mark of a professional. Preparation is also the mark of a successful person in any field. As you move upward in any occupation, you will find that the top people spend far more time in preparation than the average person does. The top 10 percent in any field are always more thoroughly prepared in every detail than those who struggle for a living in the same occupation.

When packing for trips, professional travelers take several steps over and over until they become habits. First, they make a list of everything that they will need for the upcoming trip. They do not trust to memory. They write it all down.

Second, they lay out everything they are going to take with them, in advance, before packing. Third, they pack completely so that they are ready to leave for the airport well in advance of the scheduled time. Professional travelers know that if you pack in a panic because you have not allowed enough time, you will forget things that can lead to unnecessary inconveniences later on your journey.

One of the techniques that you can use to travel well and increase the likelihood that you will arrive at your destination is to practice "worst possible outcome" thinking. To do this, ask yourself, What is the worst possible thing that could happen on this trip?

Guard Against the Worst

For me, as a professional speaker and seminar leader, the worst thing that could happen would be for my luggage to be lost and for me to arrive without the clothes and seminar materials that I need for my speaking engagement. To guard against this situation, I carry all my essentials on board with me, never out of my sight. Because of this habit of advance planning, I have never had an insurmountable problem because of baggage delays or losses.

Even if I am taking a long trip, involving several days of travel and speaking, and I need a larger suitcase, I always carry a smaller case on board with all my essentials. The larger case can be checked, but if it gets lost in transit, the loss is merely an inconvenience, not a disaster.

On the way to your destination, in the achievement of your most important goal, continually ask yourself, What are the worst possible things that can happen? And then guard against them.

Plan for Any Eventuality

The mark of a superior thinker is that he or she assumes that the worst will happen and makes provisions against it. Napoleon Bonaparte was once asked if he believed in luck. He replied, "Yes, I do. I believe in bad luck. I believe I will always have it, and I plan accordingly."

For example, it is not uncommon for flights to be delayed or cancelled because of weather or technical problems. This has happened to me numerous times. To guard against this, I always request a list of the flights leaving before and after my scheduled flight from my travel agent. If there is a problem with the flight on which I am scheduled, I quickly transfer to another flight. On those occasions when unexpected emergencies arise, I immediately telephone my travel agent, who can pull up all alternate flights on her computer and reroute me within minutes.

Move Quickly When You Need To

Not long ago, I boarded a five-hour, cross-country flight to conduct a seminar for a Fortune 500 company. When everyone was seated, the pilot announced that there was a technical problem and that the crew was working to fix it. He said that he would give an update in about thirty minutes, and during that time, the passengers could read or make phone calls.

Having experienced this type of indeterminate delay in the past, I immediately called my travel agent from the plane, found that an alternate flight was leaving twenty minutes later from the same concourse, got up, left the plane, caught the other plane, and arrived at my destination within thirty minutes of the original scheduled time.

Later I learned that the technical problems on the first plane turned out to be far more serious than they first anticipated. The passengers were kept on the plane or in the boarding area for more than three hours, at which point the flight was cancelled. Since all other flights to the East had already departed for the day, the passengers had no choice but to go home and return the following day, if they could find a seat on another flight, to get to their destinations.

Small Setbacks Can Derail Your Plans

You may need something as simple as a taxi to get to the airport. But the longer you wait to order the taxi, the more likely it is that the taxi will be late or even unavailable. Remember the old Six-P Formula: "Proper prior planning prevents poor performance."

During an ice storm in Dallas a couple of years ago, I was forced to stay twenty-five miles from the airport in a motel at which I arrived after midnight. But I had to be back at the airport by 7:00 a.m. to catch a flight and be in Birmingham on time for my seminar.

The night clerk at the motel was obviously tired and uninterested. I emphasized to him that I needed a taxi at 5:30 a.m. to go to the airport. He assured me that he would call for the taxi and that it would be waiting for me at 5:30 the next morning. After about four hours of sleep, I arose, dressed, and hurried downstairs to get my taxi to the airport. But it wasn't there.

The same desk clerk was still on the job. When I asked him about my taxi, he shrugged his shoulders haplessly and told me that he had forgotten. I was stranded.

Fortunately, just at that moment, an airline bus came by to pick up members of the air crew for the early morning flights. I wheedled my way onto this private bus and then bribed the driver to take me to my terminal, arriving just in time to catch my flight and get to Birmingham on schedule.

Refuse to Be Passive

This experience taught me two things. First, prepare for the *worst*. No matter what anyone tells you, be prepared for the possibility that he or she will not follow through.

Second, be *proactive*, not passive. Instead of becoming angry or depressed, get busy and get going. Find an alternative. Refuse to accept the current situation if it is not satisfactory. Instead of waiting for things to happen, make things happen.

Prepare a Checklist

Pilots carefully review a checklist prior to every flight. Even if they have flown thousands of hours and have been active pilots for twenty years, they still go through the checklist every single time.

You should prepare a checklist as well. No matter how many times you have made the same trip, you should review your checklist once more. Never trust to memory. The failure to check just one critical detail can leave you stranded and maybe even put your destination out of reach.

Some years ago, I did a series of seminars for IBM. One of my clients within IBM, an excellent manager and a really nice guy, suddenly stopped returning my calls. When I contacted other people in the company, I found that he had died in a plane crash while on a business trip. What had happened was truly tragic.

The plane had crashed on landing in Dallas, and everyone on board perished. In the investigation that took place later, the cause of the crash was discovered. It was the last flight of the day, and the crew was looking forward to an evening in Dallas. According to the black box, the crew members were chatting away happily as they approached the runway to land. The flight engineer—a man with two decades of experience—while chatting with the pilots in the cockpit, failed to review his checklist. As a result, he forgot to put down the flaps as the plane landed. This one mistake caused the plane to crash, burst into flames, and kill everyone on board.

As you proceed toward your personal destinations, and struggle toward your goals, the consequences of not following your checklist will not be as severe. But it is not unusual for a business to go broke or a person to lose all his or her money because someone failed to pay attention to a critical detail.

The Keys to Preparation

You have heard it said that "well begun is half done." Preparation is the mark of all professionals and successful people in every area. The way to prepare effectively is to follow your own personal checklist. Here are some suggested steps:

1. Where are you going? Take the time to be absolutely clear about your goals and dreams. Where do you want to end up? What would your situation look like if everything were perfect? The greater clarity you have concerning your final result, the easier it will be to plan the interim steps.

2. Make a list of everything that you can think of that you will have to do to achieve your goal, to reach your destination. Leave nothing out. Continue to add to the list as you think of new actions you could take.

3. Imagine every possible thing that could go wrong or that could cause delays or failure on your way toward your goal. Think ahead and make provisions against the unexpected. Never trust to luck or hope that everything will work out exactly as you planned.

4. Talk to others who have taken the same journey. Don't try to reinvent the wheel. Ask humbly for advice from people who have already paid the price to get to where you want to go.

5. Read everything you can that others have written about your route and your destination. Sometimes, a single insight from a single person can make all the difference between success and failure.

The more important your goal or destination is to you, your family, and your future, the more time you should spend in preparation before you make an irreversible commitment. There is no such word as "overprepare."

Develop a Plan B

When you set off for your goal or destination, take the time to identify the possible delays, distractions, and detours on your route. Always develop a "Plan B" in case your first plan doesn't work out. Never assume that everything will turn out the way you expect.

In business, you should identify the essential people, customers, sources of finance, marketing and selling methods, and other factors that are critical to starting and running your business successfully. In your personal life, you should also think about the worst possible things that could happen to frustrate or derail your plans. Develop a Plan B just in case.

Never forget Murphy's Laws:

1. Whatever can go wrong will go wrong.

2. The worst thing that can go wrong will go wrong at the worst possible time.

3. The worst thing that can cost the most money will go wrong at the worst possible time.

And then there is Cohen's Law: "Murphy was an optimist."

Plan and Prepare in Advance

Your ability to be absolutely clear about your perfect destination or goal and then to think through and plan every detail before you start your journey can dramatically reduce the uncertainty involved and increase the probability that you will achieve exactly the goal that you have set for yourself. Remember the saying "Well begun is half done."

Successful people are aware of the important details, especially at the beginning of a new venture or journey. They leave nothing to chance. They do not assume that everything will be done correctly or that anyone else cares about their journey as much as they do. As a result, they dramatically increase the probability that they will achieve their goals, and it has nothing at all to do with luck.

CHAPTER FIVE

Take Off at Full Throttle

**There can be no great courage where
there is no confidence or assurance,
and half the battle is in the conviction
that we can do what we undertake.**

ORISON SWETT MARDEN

Y ou have decided on your destination, arrived at
the airport, boarded the plane, and taken your
seat. You are now ready for the most important
step of all: the takeoff, the launch, where you step out in
faith with no guarantee of success. This is the turning
point in your life and in the life of every successful person.

The plane taxies to the runway, gets clearance for
takeoff from the tower, and starts down the runway. This
is the critical moment, the takeoff that is the true beginning of your journey toward your destination.

Once the plane has clearance, the pilot gives the plane 100 percent full throttle. The plane begins moving, slowly at first, and then picks up speed, going faster and faster down the runway until it lifts off into the air. This is the moment that pilots call "wheels up." It is the official beginning of the flight.

Here is a key question: What if the pilot, instead of going at full throttle, decided to use only 80 or 90 percent throttle? Any pilot will give you the answer. If the plane went at any less than full throttle, it would never reach takeoff speed. The plane would keep going until it ran out of runway without ever rising into the air.

This illustrates a key difference between success and mediocrity in life. Successful people take off at full throttle when they embark on a new flight toward a new destination. They work full blast at their jobs. They throw their whole hearts into whatever they are doing, especially at the beginning of any new endeavor.

Perhaps nothing is more important in achieving the success you desire than for you to be prepared to work very, very hard for a long time until you achieve your goal.

Average people, on the other hand, never fly at full throttle. They look for ways to take it easy, to do as little as possible. As a result, they never achieve liftoff. They never get into the air. They never really succeed at anything.

Take the First Step

The primary difference between greatness and mediocrity in life is this: great people set a big, exciting goal for themselves, plan their steps to the goal in detail, and then *take the first step.*

Average people have hopes, dreams, wishes, and desires—the same as successful people. But at the moment of truth, average people hold back. Something inside blocks them from taking the first step. Their fears of failure and loss overwhelm them at the moment of decision, and they back off.

Many years ago, I read a quote: "On the beaches of despair lie the bleached bones of those who, at the moment of triumph, hesitated, and in hesitating lost all." I never forgot it.

Courage Is the Key

The critical ingredient that you need to succeed greatly is *courage.* As Winston Churchill wrote, "Courage is rightly considered the foremost of the virtues, for upon it, all others depend." Margaret Thatcher, the "Iron Lady of Britain," once said that everything comes down to courage at the sticking point.

Robert Greene, author of the book *Power,* said, "Always be audacious. Audacity will often get you into trouble, but even more audacity will get you out."

Go as Far as You Can See

You must be clear about your goal but be *flexible* about the process of achieving it. No matter how well you plan and organize in advance, unforeseen circumstances will force you to revise your plans over and over again. But you must be prepared to take the first step.

Fortunately, you can always see far enough to take the first step. Nature is a joker in this sense, holding a blanket over the path. Once you decide upon a goal or destination, Nature will move back and show you the first step. This is a test. Nature determines whether you are really serious or not by showing the first step.

When you step out in faith, even though you can see only a single step ahead, Nature will conclude that you are serious. She will then move back and reveal the next step. And when you take that step, Nature will move back again and show you one more step. You will always be able to see one more step, and when you take it, you will see far enough to go further.

The Pursuit of Excellence

The equivalent of taking off at full throttle in your life and work is, first of all, resolving to work very hard until you achieve the success you desire. And second, it is becoming excellent at what you do. To fulfill your true potential, you must resolve in advance to be the best, to join the top 10 percent of people in your field. All the happiness, rewards, satisfaction, and recognition go to the people at the top. The rest of the people simply share whatever is left over.

Gary Becker, the 1992 Nobel Prize–winning economist, wrote an article recently about the "inequality gap" in America. He demonstrated that "the so-called inequality gap is really a skills gap." Because we live in a high-tech, knowledge-based society, more and more rewards go to those who continually upgrade their knowledge and skills. The highest incomes go to those who are continually learning new ways to add more value.

The More You Put In, the More You Get Out

In addition, higher-income households contain more employed people who work longer hours than lower-income households. The average entrepreneur, business owner, or senior executive in the upper income brackets works fifty-nine hours per week. In the lower 20 percent of households, based on income, the residents work less than twenty hours per week. Remember, you cannot reap what you do not sow.

In *The Millionaire Next Door*, authors Stanley and Danko found, in twenty-five years of interviews, that more than 85 percent of the self-made millionaires attributed their success to hard work. They repeatedly said something like "I didn't have a great education. I wasn't smarter or better than anyone else, but I was willing to work harder than they were."

The people in the top 10 percent of their fields earn two times, five times, ten times, and even twenty times as much as the average of the people in the bottom 80 percent of the same field. The top 10 percent is where you want to be sometime in the future, if you are not there already.

Work All the Time You Work

Following one rule will guarantee that you achieve your goals and reach your destination: Work all the time you work. When you go to work, *work*. Don't waste time fooling around or socializing. Work all day long. Resolve to start a little earlier, work a little harder, and stay a little later. Work all the time you work.

Stay away from people who are time wasters. Most of the people around you are working at half speed or less. They want to talk about family, sports, politics, and other nonbusiness issues. Get away from them and keep away from them. Tell them that you would love to talk with them after work, but right now, you have to get back to work.

Make a list of tasks for each day, organized by priorities. Start on your most important task first thing in the morning, and stay with it until it is 100 percent complete. Resolve to develop a reputation as the hardest working person in your company. *Work all the time you work.*

Success is not an accident. Success is completely predictable. If you do what other successful people do, over and over, you will eventually get the same results that they do. Nothing can hold you back but yourself.

CHAPTER SIX

Plan for Turbulence

If I were asked to give what I consider the single most useful piece of advice for all humanity it would be this: Expect trouble as an inevitable part of life and when it comes, hold your head high, look it squarely in the eye, and say, "I will be bigger than you. You cannot defeat me."

ANN LANDERS

O n a flight, when your plane takes off, the pilot tells all the passengers to stay in their seats with their seatbelts buckled. In many cases, the pilot will say, "We expect a certain amount of turbulence for the first part of the flight, so please stay buckled up."

When you start any new business or job, you will experience turbulence as well. The first phase of any job, business, or new venture usually plunges you into a series of unexpected problems and difficulties that you never imagined you would encounter. It's very much like a plane hitting a downdraft and being put into a dive.

As soon as you commit to your new goal and take the plunge, everything that possibly can go wrong will go wrong. You will learn more lessons in the first few days after starting a new venture than you may have learned or thought of in a year of planning and organizing.

When you start toward a new goal, you will make a continual series of mistakes, all of which will cost time, money, and emotion. There is no other way to develop the knowledge, skills, and character you need to succeed except by making mistakes and learning from experience.

Your journey toward your destination will consist of a series of problems, reversals, and temporary failures. They are an unavoidable part of life. No success is possible without your developing the ability to deal with and overcome the inevitable challenges and obstacles between you and anything you are trying to accomplish.

Control Your Responses

Strong people expect to experience problems on their journey toward their goals and destinations. Weak people are surprised and dismayed when things don't work out the way they had expected. They become angry and lash out. They blame other people for their problems. Often they become depressed or irrational.

You can influence only one part of the problem equation: the way that you *respond* to difficulties as they come along. This is often called your "response-ability."

Your success in life is largely determined by your ability to respond effectively to problems as they come up. Fortunately, you can learn a number of effective strategies practiced by successful people to deal with problems.

Problems Go with the Territory

First of all, *expect* to have problems, disappointments, and temporary failures. Don't be shocked, surprised, or angry when they occur. Instead, take a deep breath, relax, and say, "Solving problems is my job; problems are what I do."

Each time you solve a problem, you will become even more capable of solving even greater problems. The major reward you get for solving problems is the opportunity to solve even bigger problems. But with bigger problems come bigger rewards and responsibilities.

You will always rise to the height of your ability to deal with the problems in your work and personal life. Big people solve big problems. Little people solve little problems or no problems at all. The most successful and confident people in every area are those who have effectively dealt with the greatest number of problems, large and small, in their fields.

Think in Terms of Solutions

Superior people are intensely solution oriented. They think about solutions and what can be done rather than the problems and who is to blame. They are future oriented and continually think in terms of the actions that they can take immediately to control the damage, minimize the problem, and move ahead.

One of the best strategies you can use is to practice mental preparation with regard to problems. Resolve in advance that no matter what happens, you will remain calm and relaxed. Resolve in advance that you will not become upset or angry. Preprogram yourself mentally to deal with problems in a calm and effective manner.

When you have preprogrammed yourself in this way and the inevitable problem situation arrives, you will find yourself automatically slowing down and becoming calmer. You will be more relaxed and objective. You will take control of the situation.

Ask Questions

When you deal with unexpected turbulence in your business or personal life, you can keep yourself calm, clear, and focused by asking questions rather than reacting or overreacting.

First of all, get the facts. What exactly is the problem? How did it occur? What are the exact costs or dimensions of the problem? Be sure to double-check your facts. Very often, what seems to be a problem will turn out to be exaggerated or based on incorrect information.

Sometimes, the solution to the problem is contained within the problem itself. It may be that when a problem occurs, it turns out not to be a problem at all. Often it can be a blessing in disguise. The very act of asking questions keeps you calm and in control. Focus on the *solution*. Ask, What actions can I or we take immediately to deal with this problem?

When faced with a problem of any kind, most people tend to "catastrophize," or think of the worst possible thing that could happen, and to look for someone to blame for what has occurred. You must resist both of these tendencies and discourage the people around you from thinking like this as well.

Accept Responsibility and Take Charge

Once you have clearly defined the problem (and confirmed that it actually is a problem) and you have thought about the various actions you can take to solve or minimize it, the next step is to either take responsibility for taking action or assign specific responsibility for taking action to someone else.

Think always in terms of the actions you can take. Just as a pilot facing unexpected turbulence keeps both hands on the wheel and his or her eyes on the gauges, when you experience problems, you must take command of your situation and ensure that you are flying in the right direction.

Every difficulty in life is a test of some kind. The only question is whether you pass or fail the test. Each time you respond effectively to a problem or difficulty, you develop greater wisdom, intelligence, and personal power. You become smarter, more competent, and more capable of solving even greater problems.

Change Your Language

In flying, the word "attitude" refers to the angle of flight or your approach relative to the horizon. The way you think about a problem determines your attitude, or approach, as well.

You can use three words to change your attitude and your approach to any difficulty you face. First of all, change the word "problem" to the word "situation." Whereas "problem" is a negative word that triggers feelings of fear and anxiety, "situation" is neutral. Instead of saying, "We have a problem," you can say, "We have a situation."

My personal preference is to change the word "problem" to the word "challenge." Whenever something goes wrong, immediately say, "We have an interesting challenge facing us today."

"Challenge" is a positive word. When you think of a challenge, you think of something that you rise to, something that brings out the best in you and others. Challenges are what make life exciting and worth living. By rising to the challenges of day-to-day life, you fulfill more and more of your potential.

Perhaps the best word of all is "opportunity." Instead of saying, "We have a problem," you can say, "We have an unexpected opportunity."

Napoleon Hill is famous for saying, "Every problem or difficulty you face contains the seed of an equal or greater advantage or benefit." Your job is to find the benefit, and this way of approaching a problem is determined by your attitude.

This attitude of looking for the good in every situation, of looking for the advantage or benefit in any problem or difficulty, is the way that the most successful people think most of the time.

Unlock Your Mental Powers

Your brain is a remarkable organ. When you are calm and relaxed, your *neocortex*, your thinking brain, is fully active and available to you. But when you become anxious or angry, your neocortex shuts down, like all the lights in a building being turned off. When you become emotional about a problem, you fall back into thinking with your *paleocortex*, which is your limbic or emotional brain.

Your emotional brain has two states: fight or flight. When you become fearful or anxious about a problem in either state, you can quite easily slip into a state of denial, anger, or blame. You may feel like lashing out and attacking, or you may want to ignore the problem and hope that it goes away by itself. But neither of these responses is helpful.

Superior people, leaders in all areas, face the inevitable ups and downs of daily life on the way to their destinations by taking complete control of their thinking and their emotions. They do this by choosing the words they use to describe a situation, their tone of voice, and their behavior in dealing with problems.

Flying into Headwinds

When you set off toward a new destination or goal, like taking off in an airplane, you will have an idea of both your departure time and your arrival time. You will set a schedule for yourself and expect to arrive pretty much on schedule. But as soon as you take off, you will experience what pilots call "unexpected headwinds."

Over the years, I have traveled many millions of miles. I have had almost every experience, except a crash. It is not unusual, especially during the spring or fall, for a plane to run into headwinds on a cross-country trip. Sometimes these headwinds can be 150 to 200 miles per hour and delay a flight by as much as two hours in the air. Once when I was flying from New York to Dallas, the headwinds were so strong and lasted so long that the pilot actually had to land in St. Louis to refuel the plane.

The situation in your own life is similar. As soon as you embark on a new journey, you will experience headwinds as well: everything will cost twice as much and take three times longer than you anticipated. In a new venture, you should make your very best financial projections and then double them to reach a realistic number. You should estimate how long you will take to achieve certain milestones and then triple that time to get the actual time period required.

Types of Headwinds

Headwinds in your business and personal life will come from several sources. Your primary source of headwinds will be *other people.* They will disappoint you, cheat you, betray you, fail to live up to your expectations, and turn out to be incompetent or indifferent. If you expect that everyone you deal with is going to be intelligent, competent, and honest, you are going to experience a considerable number of challenges on your road to wisdom and experience.

Your customers will be a major source of headwinds. When you start a new venture, you will be amazed at how difficult it is to get customers to buy your product or service for the first time. You will be astonished at how hard it is to get customers to switch from their current suppliers to buy from you. Most customers are in their own comfort zones. Following the Law of Inertia, they will continue to buy from an existing supplier, even if your product or service is superior, because they are comfortable with what they have done in the past.

Your customers will disappoint you in that they will buy less than you expected, take longer to buy than you expected, pay slower than you expected, and complain more than you expected. You will often find that the product or service that you offer to your customers to add value to their lives is overpriced, not competitive with others, and defective in terms of delivering the results or benefits that you promised. These difficulties and challenges are normal and natural. Your job is to deal with them as realities and find some way to solve them.

Remember that the customer is always right. It is not what you produce but what people buy that counts. It is not what you want to offer but what people want to enjoy that determines your future. In life, we earn our livings by serving others in some way. And those others always define what we have to do to be successful. Face the facts, deal with reality, and modify your product or service so that customers buy it, buy it again, and tell their friends.

Financial Headwinds

Another form of headwinds that you will face has to do with *money*. Some people will tell you that it is easy to make all the money you want just by thinking positively and visualizing yourself as wealthy. Everyone wants to believe that this is true, and many people embrace the idea of effortless wealth with their whole hearts.

But that doesn't include those people who have actually achieved financial success. People who have made a lot of money have learned through bitter experience that the only thing easy about money is losing it. As the Japanese proverb says, "Making money is like digging with a pin; losing money is like pouring water on the sand."

Money is a very emotional issue. People are extremely reluctant to part with their money for any reason. When you approach friends, banks, lenders, or suppliers for loans or lines of credit, you will find that they are skeptical, suspicious, slow to act, and extremely careful with their money. Because people with money have had every kind of experience, including being lied to, deceived, and cheated many times in the past, they are extremely hesitant and cautious about providing money to you, or to anyone else, for any reason.

Personal Headwinds

You will experience headwinds *personally* in that you will discover, much to your surprise, that you lack specific talents, skills, and knowledge that you need to succeed. You may find that you are a poor time manager or that you lack self-discipline. You cannot seem to focus, concentrate, and apply yourself single-mindedly to your most important tasks. You waste time and feel overwhelmed with too much to do and too little time in which to do it.

You may lack financial, analytic, marketing, or selling skills. You may not know how to plan and organize your business, advertise effectively and attract customers, or persuade your prospects to buy from you. You may not know how to attract and keep good people or to make good business decisions.

If you are starting and building a business, you may lack the ability to choose the right people for the right positions in your business. You may lack the ability to delegate to and supervise your staff to ensure that they get their jobs done on time, on budget, and to specific measures of performance.

Fortunately, these are all *learnable* skills. But the starting point of mastering these essential skills is for you to admit that you need them, that you are not particularly good in some areas. After that, your education can begin.

Because of your incredible mind, you can learn any skill you need to learn to achieve any goal you can set for yourself. You must never allow yourself to be held back simply because you lack a particular skill or ability. Instead, you must set the development of that skill as a goal, make a plan to achieve it, and then work on it every day until you have mastered that skill.

Don't Be Surprised

A mark of maturity, a vital quality to develop on the road to success, happiness, and balance in life, is expecting problems and difficulties as normal, natural, and unavoidable parts of life. Becoming a superior person requires accepting that when you set off toward a big, exciting goal or destination, you will experience unexpected turbulence and headwinds continually. Your job is to learn to navigate through these difficulties with calmness, clarity, and complete self-confidence.

You become a calm, effective thinker by remaining calm in the face of any adversity. You become patient by practicing patience whenever it is called for. You become a superb pilot of your own destiny by dealing effectively with the inevitable storms that occur in your work and personal life.

CHAPTER SEVEN

Make Continual Course Corrections

**Sooner or later comes a crisis in our affairs,
and how we meet it determines our
future happiness and success. Since the
beginning of time, every form of life has
been called upon to meet such a crisis.**

ROBERT COLLIER

P roblems, difficulties, and setbacks are a normal, natural, and unavoidable part of life and business. When you set a new goal or launch toward a new destination, you will experience challenges and difficulties that you never expected or anticipated. But the true test of character is the inevitable and unavoidable *crisis*. Your ability to solve problems is important, but your ability to deal with crises largely determines your success or failure in life.

It is estimated that the average person today experiences a crisis every two to three months. This can be a business crises, financial crisis, family crisis, physical crisis, or personal crisis of some kind. This means that each person you know, including yourself, is either in a crisis today, has just gotten out of a crisis, or is just about to have a crisis.

Crises, by their very definition, come unbidden. They are completely unexpected, from out of left field. And since you cannot predict or anticipate a crisis, the only thing you can do when one occurs is to respond to it effectively.

Leadership Abilities

In a multiyear study conducted at Stanford University, researchers examined the annual performance appraisals of hundreds of presidents and chief executive officers of Fortune 1000 companies, some of the most successful executives in every business or industry. The experts looked at what had been written about the executives from the time they started work, searching for the common characteristics of top people.

This study revealed that top executives had two dominant qualities in common. The first was the ability to function well as a member of a team. When they were starting out, they were good team players, making valuable contributions to the teams they were on. As they were promoted to more senior positions, they demonstrated an ability to bring together winning teams of talented people and organize them to accomplish important goals and results for their companies.

The Most Important Leadership Quality

The second, and most important, quality that top leaders had in common was the ability to function well in a crisis. Top people in every field had demonstrated throughout their careers that they were able to deal effectively with the inevitable crisis when it came along.

The researchers discovered something else: teamwork could be taught in seminars and workshops. But the ability to function well in a crisis was not teachable. A leader did not learn to deal with crises in a workshop or seminar or by role-playing with other people in an imaginary problem situation.

The ability to deal with a crisis could be learned and demonstrated only in a *real* crisis, an unpredictable and unexpected reversal or setback that had the potential to cause major damage of some kind. During such a crisis, the true leader would emerge to save the situation and resolve the problem.

Life Is a Series of Tests

In life, problems are the tests you must pass to move onward and upward. The inevitable crises that you experience in your day-to-day life are the true tests of your competence and your maturity. They are the measure of your character. They are the best indicator of the levels of courage, intelligence, persistence, and foresight that you have developed up to this moment.

As Epictetus said, "Circumstances do not make the man; they merely reveal him to himself." And to others, for that matter.

When you are a leader faced with a crisis, everyone watches you to see how you react. Everyone measures and judges. People upgrade or downgrade you in their estimation. The crisis is the great "crunch time" of life.

How Leaders Perform in a Crisis

Over the years, I have worked with the presidents and chief executive officers of many large companies. I have coached, counseled, and consulted with millionaires, multimillionaires, and even billionaires. I have been able to watch them "up close and personal."

One quality that they all seemed to demonstrate was their ability to remain calm and cool when faced with a major reversal or setback. When they were confronted with a problem or crisis, they seemed to be able to turn on a switch in their minds that enabled them to become calm and completely in control. They immediately took charge of their emotions and the situation.

The top people I have dealt with never became angry or upset. They did not become excited or irritated. In fact, they seemed to go to the opposite extreme. They slowed down and became more polite and courteous. They said "Please" and "Thank you." They asked questions and gathered information before reacting or responding.

Get the Facts

Harold Geneen, the past president of IT&T, a 150-company conglomerate, once said that the most important step in dealing with any business problem was to get the facts. He said, "Get the real facts. Not the assumed facts, the apparent facts, the obvious facts, or the hoped-for facts. Keep digging until you get the real facts. Facts don't lie."

Whenever Jack Welch, former CEO of General Electric, was presented with a problem, he would ask, "What's the reality?" He insisted on knowing the truth about the situation, whatever it was.

These executives found that the more information (the greater number of facts) that they gathered about any problem or crisis, the more obvious would be the correct solution or course of action. This solution would seem to emerge as the result of delving deeper and deeper into the problem.

The Most Important Work

What is the most important work you do? The answer is "thinking." Your ability to think clearly and make good decisions largely determines the course and quality of

your life. People who think better come to better conclusions. They take better actions and get better results. People who do not take the time to properly think through
situations often come to the wrong conclusions, make the
wrong decisions, and take the wrong actions, leading to
underachievement and failure over and over again.

The most valuable skill you bring to your life and your
work is your ability to think calmly and clearly. This requires that you deliberately practice a form of detach-
ment when you are dealing with an unexpected reversal.
You remain objective. You imagine that you are a consultant who has been brought in from the outside to analyze
this problem or crisis and make recommendations. You
hold it at arm's length while you are examining the situation. You remain unemotional while you collect information. Only when you feel that you have learned everything
you can about the problem do you make your recommendations and decisions.

Think Ahead

One of the most important thinking skills that you can
develop is crisis anticipation. To practice this skill, regularly look down the road of life, into the future, and ask
yourself, What are the worst possible things that could go
wrong? What could derail my plans or block my ability to
achieve my goals?

Make a list of every problem or crisis that could occur.
Use the 3 percent rule: Even if a serious problem has only

a 3 percent chance of occurring, write it down on your list. Think about what would happen if it occurred and how you would respond.

Royal Dutch Shell, one of the biggest oil companies in the world, is famous for its scenario planning. Because it has oil and gas fields, pumping stations, pipelines, ships, refineries, and gas stations around the world, the company has developed more than six hundred scenarios to deal with various crises, should they occur.

As a result, if there is a pipeline breakdown in Kazakhstan, a civil war in Nigeria, or an oil spill in Alaska, Royal Dutch Shell has a written plan of action to respond to the situation. The company is prepared to react quickly and efficiently, minimizing damages and costs, shifting oil and gas from one place to another to avoid disruption of supplies.

In the same way, you should project into the future and think about what could happen to disrupt your plans or block you from achieving your goals. You then return to the present and ask, If such a situation were to happen, what would I do immediately to deal with it?

The Key to Victory

Napoleon Bonaparte was famous for his ability to antici-pate what might happen in the course of a battle. He would ride out in advance with his generals and inspect the potential battlefield. He would study the lay of the land carefully, noting where he could deploy his artillery, mass his infantry, and move his cavalry. Then, whenever possible, he would lure the enemy army onto the battle-field of his own choosing.

Today, we remember Napoleon as the general who lost at the Battle of Waterloo. He also lost at the Battle of Leipzig in Germany in 1813, and he failed in his invasion of Russia in 1812. But what is often forgotten is that between 1793 and 1815, he led the French armies in hun-dreds of battles, all over Europe, and was victorious almost every time, often against superior forces.

His ability to practice crisis anticipation, to foresee the worst possible things that could happen in any battle, gave him a tremendous edge over the enemy general. No matter what happened when the firing began, he was ready. As the battle unfolded, he could immediately give orders to deal with an unexpected enemy action or take advantage of a withdrawal or breakthrough. He had thought through every possible scenario in advance.

The greater thought that you have given to the possi-ble problems, challenges, and crises that you may face, in advance, the calmer and more confident you will be when they actually occur. And just as summer follows spring, your life will be an endless series of problems and crises, large and small.

Making Course Corrections

This brings us to one of the most important parts of the real secret of success. Earlier I said that an airplane is off course 99 percent of the time. Every flight from one place to another requires a continual series of course corrections to keep the plane flying toward its destination.

In your life, you will have to make continual course corrections as well. Every hour of every day, you will have to make major and minor changes to deal with unexpected events and circumstances. Your ability to make these course corrections quickly and effectively will determine your success more than any other single factor.

Resist the Lure of the Comfort Zone

Because of the fear of failure, the majority of people resist change, even if the change is to their benefit. Because of the Law of Inertia—"A body in motion tends to remain in motion unless acted upon by an outside force"—people tend to keep doing the same things, day after day and year after year, for no other reason than they are comfortable doing them in a particular way.

Harold Geneen said, "The biggest problem in the executive suite is not alcoholism or workaholism; it is egoism."

Most people hate to be wrong. Even if it is clear they are wrong, they hate to admit it. Because of their egos, they go through incredible mental and emotional gyrations to avoid admitting that they have made a mistake. If they are caught in a mistake, most people tend to ignore it, deny it, or blame it on someone else. They refuse to make course corrections.

Change Is the Only Constant

But in times of rapid change, according to the American Management Association, you are going to be wrong at least 70 percent of the time. Information will change. Technology will advance. Your competition will do something unexpected. Events over which you have no control can render your best plans and intentions worthless.

On Friday, you may put together a complete plan of action, involving many days or weeks of planning. But then on Monday, something may happen in the marketplace—as big as 9/11 or as small as a price reduction by your competitor—that changes all your plans.

This is why *flexibility* is an essential quality that you must develop for dealing effectively with the storms, turbulence, headwinds, and lightning that you experience on your flight toward your destination. You must be willing to accept feedback and to self-correct. You must be more concerned with what's right than who's right.

Some people think that to admit mistakes and change direction is a sign of weakness or incompetence. But in times of rapid change, the willingness to admit that you are not perfect, that you have new information that requires that you change your course of action, is a mark of courage, character, and personal strength. Weak people always attempt to cover up their mistakes. Strong people admit them quickly and then immediately take a different course of action.

Keep your mind clear by practicing *zero-based thinking* at all times. Ask yourself, Based on this new information, if I were not now doing this, knowing what I now know, would I start it up again today?

If the answer is no, immediately make whatever changes are necessary to keep on course toward your goal. Remember this rule: Be clear about your goal, but be flexible about the process of achieving it.

Take Control of Your Mind

Whenever you are hit with an unavoidable crisis, take control of your mind—and the situation—by asking yourself and others these key questions:

1. What are we trying to do?

2. How are we trying to do it?

3. Is there a better way?

4. What are our assumptions?

5. What if our assumptions were wrong?

6. What actions should we take immediately based on our answers to these questions?

7. What is the first action we should take?

Separate facts from problems. A fact is something that is fixed and immovable, like a past event that you cannot change or a current event over which you have no control, like the weather.

On the other hand, a problem is something that can be solved. You can do something about it. You can apply your mind to finding a solution of some kind.

The rule is simple: Refuse to become upset or angry about something that you cannot change. Save your time and energy for those challenges you can influence in some way. Remind yourself that "what cannot be cured must be endured."

How to Remain Flexible

You can make three statements on a regular basis to clear your mind and increase your ability to deal with any situation. When you develop the habit of making these statements in response to problems and difficulties, you will much more easily make the course corrections that are essential to reaching your destination.

1. When you make a decision, and new information or circumstances prove that it was the wrong decision, don't be afraid to say, "**I was wrong.**"

   As soon as you admit that you were wrong, the situation is over. You don't have to waste another minute or ounce of energy defending, justifying, or explaining yourself. Simply say, "I was wrong," and start determining the course corrections you need to make based on your new information.

2. The second statement you can make is "**I made a mistake.**"

Since fully 70 percent of your decisions will turn out to be wrong, your entire life will be dotted with a series of large and small mistakes. When you can calmly and confidently admit that you are not perfect, that based on the information you had you came to the wrong conclusion and you made a mistake, the situation is over. Everyone can now focus on the solution and what actions you can take to get back on course.

3. The third statement you can make is "I changed my mind."

Throughout your life, you are going to make decisions based on how you think and feel at the moment. But after a few hours or a few days, you may see the situation differently. You may realize that based on your current information, your previous decision was not the best one for you. When you have the strength to simply admit that you have changed your mind, you can move on.

Free to Choose

My parents were very rigid in their thinking. Once they had taken a position, they would never budge. As a result, my life as a child was frustrating. Even if they were wrong, my parents would never admit it because their egos were involved.

When I raised my children, I decided to reverse this behavior. I told them from an early age, "You are always free to change your mind." I didn't want them to ever feel that if they had made a statement or taken a position, they were trapped into defending it for the indefinite future.

My daughter Christina, who is now grown and married, has told me repeatedly that this advice, "You are always free to change your mind," has been one of the most liberating ideas she ever learned. She teaches it to everyone. You can practice it for yourself.

The key to achieving everything that is possible for you is to make continual course corrections throughout your life. And you can always change your mind.

CHAPTER EIGHT

Accelerate Your Learning and Progress

It is only with the heart that one can see rightly;
what is essential is invisible to the eye.

ANTOINE DE SAINT-EXUPÉRY

What is your most valuable financial asset? Surprisingly enough, it is not your home, your investments, or your bank account. It is your *earning ability*. Your ability to earn money is the most precious and perishable asset you have.

It has taken you your entire life to develop your earning ability to the level it is today. Your current earning ability is a combination of your knowledge, skills, experience, education, background, personality, character, and qualities of thought and behavior, such as courage, self-discipline and persistence. By applying your earning

ability judiciously, you can earn tens of thousands of dollars each year.

You could lose your house, your car, your money, and
all your other material possessions. But as long as you still
have your earning ability, you can walk into the marketplace and earn them all back again.

Your Intangible Assets

Your earning ability is invisible. It is intangible. It is hard
to estimate or measure. Two people with the same IQ and
grades could graduate from the same college with the
same education and begin work at the same time. Ten
years later, one of those people has been promoted several times and is earning five or ten times as much as the
other. Why does this happen?

The explanation is simple. Your earning ability can be
an *appreciating asset* or a *depreciating asset*: it can increase in value or decrease in value over time. And this is
completely under your control.

An appreciating asset becomes more valuable as time
passes. When you dedicate yourself to lifelong learning,
to continually increasing your knowledge and skills and
your ability to add value wherever you happen to be, your
earning ability will appreciate. You will get paid more
because you become worth more. By the Law of Cause
and Effect, as you increase your earning ability, you
increase the value of your contribution and your value in a
competitive marketplace.

The Highest Paid Intelligence

According to Howard Gardner at Harvard University, the most important and highest paid intelligence in our society is *social intelligence*. This refers to your ability to negotiate; communicate; persuade; and sell yourself, your products, and your services to others.

To accomplish anything worthwhile in life, you have to have the help and cooperation of lots of people. Your *interpersonal* skills are more valuable than anything else in gaining the help and support of others, and they may be underdeveloped.

You may lack the ability to negotiate on behalf of yourself and your business and to get the very best prices when you're buying or selling. You may lack the ability to sell yourself or your products and services to skeptical consumers who are quite content with what they are currently using.

Step on Your Own Accelerator

Increasing your knowledge and skills is like using high-octane fuel in your engine on the way to your destination. Learning new skills that can increase your contribution is like stepping on the accelerator of your own potential. Simply put, to earn more, you must first learn more. As basketball coach Pat Riley said, "If you're not getting better, you're getting worse."

Unfortunately for most people, their earning ability is a fixed or, even worse, a *depreciating* asset. Their ability to contribute is not increasing at much more than the rate of inflation, about 3 percent per year. Because of this, most people just have a "job," which stands for "just over broke."

The top 20 percent of people in our society are continually increasing their earning ability, their ability to contribute more and better results to their own company or to their employers. They read the best books, listen to the best educational CDs, watch educational DVDs, and take additional courses in their fields. They pursue learning as if their future depended upon it, because it does.

Write Out the Lessons You Learn

A friend of mine started a marketing business in his twenties. He worked twelve hours a day, seven days a week, for two years, but the business failed and he lost everything.

Then he did something that changed his life. He sat down with a spiral notebook, and at the top of each page, he wrote one of a series of questions:

1. What lessons have I learned about business in general from this experience?

2. What lessons have I learned about customers and markets from this business failure?

3. What lessons have I learned about people and employees from this experience?

4. What lessons have I learned about partners and business associates?

5. What lessons have I learned about money, banking, and finances?

6. What lessons have I learned about myself and my strengths and weaknesses?

7. What lessons have I learned about producing and delivering products and services from this experience?

He then wrote a full page of answers to each of these questions, as is done in Mindstorming. This spiral notebook became his handbook for his next business venture. Every time he had a problem or difficulty, he referred to the proper page to remind himself of the lessons he had learned.

By the time he was thirty-five, he was a millionaire. By the time he was forty, he was a multimillionaire. By the time he was fifty, he retired to a beautiful home on a golf course in Palm Springs, where he lives to this day.

Achieving Personal Excellence

Personal excellence is perhaps the most important of all invisible and intangible assets that you can acquire.

Achieving personal excellence in your business or industry requires lifelong dedication. But once you get into the
top 10 percent of your field, you will be one of the highest
paid people in the country. You will enjoy the respect and
esteem of all the people around you. You will be able to
live your life the way you want to live it. You will enjoy
high levels of self-esteem, self-respect, and personal
pride.

A gentleman came up to me at a seminar in Las Vegas
not long ago. He said, "When you spoke to this company
four years ago, you told us that if we had clear written
goals, worked continually to upgrade our skills, and never
gave up, we could double our income.

"Well," he said, "you were off by a long shot. I followed your instructions to the letter. I have been working
on myself almost every single day for the last four years.
But I didn't just double my income; I have increased my
income by almost ten times. Even I have a hard time
believing how much money I am making today in comparison to what I was earning before I dedicated myself to
getting better every day at what I do."

Build Your Intellectual Assets

Each person has or can acquire three forms of intellectual
capital. These require an investment of study and hard
work, but they pay off in higher income for the rest of
your life.

The first type of intellectual capital you can acquire consists of your core knowledge, skills, and abilities. These are the result of education, experience, and training. They determine how well you do your job and the value of your contribution to your business. They can be increased and improved almost without limit throughout your life. Sometimes, the addition of one key skill can *double* the value of your contribution and your income.

Build Your Internal Knowledge

The second form of intellectual capital that you possess is your knowledge of how your business operates internally, in comparison to that of your competitors or any other business.

Each business develops a series of systems, procedures, methods, techniques, and strategies to market, sell, produce, deliver products and services, and satisfy customers. Each business or organization has its own political and social structure, its pecking order, which determines the relative importance and power of each person and whom you have to work with to get things done.

Each business has internal systems for accounting, administration, and financial controls. These systems take many years to develop and considerable time for a new person to learn. Nonetheless, they are often a key part of the "stock in trade" of the company. A person who knows and understands these systems intimately has a form of intellectual capital that is difficult for the company to replace.

When my executive assistant of fifteen years comes to me and asks for a salary increase, I realize immediately that to replace her would cost me a lot in terms of time, effort, and expense. It might take months or even years for a new person to acquire her intellectual capital. Her detailed knowledge of every aspect of my business, including customers, contacts, contracts, communications, and the complexities of my business activities, has taken her years to acquire. Giving her a raise is easy when I compare it to the cost of replacing her with someone else. She has made herself extremely valuable.

Build Your Ability to Get Results

The third form of intellectual capital that you possess, and that is perhaps the key determinant of your earning ability, is your knowledge and understanding of how you can get financial results in a competitive market. This includes your knowledge of your products and services and how to sell them. It includes your knowledge of customers and suppliers and how to deal with them. It embraces your familiarity with bankers, lawyers, accountants, and government officials and how to interact with them effectively. This form of intellectual capital may take years to build, and it is extremely valuable to your organization.

Your first responsibility to yourself is to develop your earning ability to a high level. You do this by continually increasing your intellectual capital, by upgrading your ability to do your job, by becoming a valuable part of your organization, and by getting more and better financial results for your organization.

Your Efficiency and Effectiveness

Your goal is to first make yourself valuable and then make yourself *indispensable*. The way you do this is to start a little earlier, work a little harder, and stay a little later. You become indispensable by getting more and better results than anyone else in your position. As you get a reputation for making a valuable contribution, you will quickly come to the attention of people who can help you move ahead. You will be paid more and promoted faster at every stage of your career, whether running your own business or working for someone else.

Chance Favors the Prepared Mind

You can improve your ability to capitalize on the invisible influences that can help you succeed greatly. The key is to continually take in new information. Read the books, magazines, and newsletters produced by the experts in your field. Attend the annual meetings of your industry association and learn everything you can from the experts in your business. Meet regularly with other people who work in your business and trade ideas with them.

By the Law of Probability, you can never know which idea will be the breakthrough idea that saves you years of hard work in achieving a certain level of success. You must therefore expose yourself to as many ideas and as much information as possible to increase the probability that you will have the right idea for the right situation at the right time.

The Top 10 Percent in Your Field

To achieve all that is possible for you in your chosen career, you must dedicate yourself to getting into the top 10 percent. This idea comes as a shock to many people. When I first learned that to succeed greatly, I would have to be in the top 10 percent in my field, my initial reaction was disappointment and discouragement. I had not graduated from high school. I had worked at laboring jobs for several years before I got into sales. I had been fired and laid off multiple times and had been broke or nearly broke well into my thirties.

Then I learned something that changed my life: everyone who is in the top 10 percent today started in the bottom 10 percent. Everyone who is doing well today was once doing poorly. As speaker T. Harv Eker says, "Every master was once a disaster."

Everyone Starts at the Bottom

Just think! Everyone who is at the top of your field today was at one time not in your field at all and did not even know that it existed. Today they are at the top and earn-ing several times the average income. And the best news is, whatever countless other people have done, you can do as well if you simply learn how.

No one is better than you and no one is smarter than you. You have more talent, ability, and intelligence than you could use in one hundred lifetimes. By the Law of Cause and Effect, if you learn and practice what other successful people are doing, you will eventually master the same skills that they have and get the same results that they do. There are no limits except those that you impose on your-self with your own thinking.

Here is the tragedy: the absence of a commitment to excellence becomes, by default, an acceptance of medi-ocrity. No one ever became excellent accidentally. Like achieving any long-term, worthwhile goal, becoming ex-cellent at what you do takes a long, long time.

The Achievement of Mastery

How long will it take for you to get to the top of your field? In more than fifty years of study into the subject of mastery, the experts have determined that it takes ap-proximately seven years, or ten thousand hours, of hard, focused effort for someone to get into the top 10 percent of any field.

It takes seven years to become an excellent neuro-surgeon. It takes seven years to become a top salesperson. It takes seven years to become a successful entrepreneur.

It takes seven years to become a top diesel mechanic. Whatever your chosen profession, it takes about seven years to get to the top.

When I share this with my audiences, they often react with disappointment and dismay. But the facts are the facts. Perhaps you can beat the averages, but don't bet on it. The reason that it takes seven years or ten thousand hours of hard work is because that is the length of time necessary for you to master your craft, to become truly excellent at whatever you do.

The Time Is Going to Pass Anyway

Sometimes people will say, "Wait a minute! I'm thirty years old right now. What you are saying is that I will be thirty-seven years old before I get into the top 10 percent and start to enjoy the big rewards in this field. Do you realize that I will be seven years older?"

I then ask a simple question, "How much older will you be in seven years in any case? Seven years from now, you will be seven years older than you are today. The only question is, Will you be at the top of your field, or will you still be in the bottom 80 percent, earning an average living, and worrying about money most of the time?"

The same rule applies to business success. According to a study of 30,000 businesses by a major accounting firm, a new business loses money for the first two years. In the next two years, it earns enough money to pay back the losses from the first two years. At the end of the fourth year, the business starts to earn net profits. Only in the seventh year does the business begin to take off, often making more money in a year than it made in the previous five to seven years. As Peter Drucker said, "No new business makes a profit within the first four years."

Put Yourself onto the Fast Track

So, how do you reach cruising altitude as quickly and as predictably as possible? The answer is simple: knowledge, skill, and hard work.

Dedicate yourself to continuous learning, to nonstop personal and professional development. Read in your field daily, listen to educational CDs in your car, attend seminars to learn new skills, and take additional live and online courses. Never stop learning and upgrading your knowledge.

Turn this knowledge into skill by continuous practice. Realize in advance that most new techniques that you try won't work the first time. Be prepared to work at the new skill until you master it, no matter how long it takes.

Learning a new skill is like learning how to prepare a new dish at home. No matter how good it tastes when prepared by an expert cook, your first attempts will not be as successful. But when you practice with a new recipe, continually adjusting the ingredients and changing the way that you prepare it, eventually the dish will taste delicious. From that point onward, you can prepare that dish in a superb fashion every single time.

It is the same with any business skill. At first, you will be clumsy and awkward. But as you work with the skill, over and over, you will eventually master it and own it for life. This is one of the most important principles of success you'll ever learn.

CHAPTER NINE

Activate Your Superconscious Mind

A miracle is nothing more nor less than this.
Anyone who has come into a knowledge of
his true identity, of his oneness with the
all-pervading Wisdom and Power, thus makes
it possible for laws higher than the ordinary mind
knows of to be revealed to him.

RALPH WALDO TRINE

Today's wide-bodied passenger jets have the most advanced and sophisticated avionics equipment imaginable. The high-tech computers on the average passenger plane today are capable of monitoring every part and performance measure of the plane. The avionics systems, costing millions of dollars for a large plane, are so advanced that they can make the plane take off, fly, and land almost without human assistance.

Pilots, of course, are essential on every plane for three primary reasons. First, they are necessary to set the destination. They must then go through a checklist to ensure that the plane has no technical problems. They are required to taxi to the runway, take off, and achieve altitude.

Second, pilots are essential to continually check that everything in the plane is working properly and to personally make decisions regarding wind, turbulence, storm patterns, and essential course corrections.

The third reason pilots are essential is to ensure that the plane lands safely at its destination.

Fortunately, in most cases, once the coordinates for the destination are programmed into the onboard computer by the pilot and the plane reaches cruising altitude, the plane goes on autopilot and flies unerringly toward its destination, making numerous course corrections and adjustments throughout the flight. The pilot can relax a little, knowing that millions of dollars of sophisticated technology are controlling and directing the plane toward its destination.

Your Superconscious Mind: Your Greatest Power

In the same way, your superconscious mind serves as your personal advanced avionics and guidance system. To use this mind, you first determine your exact destination or goal. You write it down, thereby programming it into your subconscious mind. When your goal is clear to your subconscious mind, it is passed over to your superconscious mind, which then works on it twenty-four hours a day until your goal is achieved and your destination is reached.

The superconscious mind has been known and talked about throughout human history. Mystics and religious teachers have called it the "God Mind." Ralph Waldo Emerson called it the "oversoul." Carl Jung referred to it as the "collective unconscious." Napoleon Hill referred to it as "Infinite Intelligence." He concluded that the ability to activate it was the primary reason for the success of the wealthiest people in America. It is also referred to as "intuition," "gut feeling," "instinct," or "the inner voice."

It doesn't matter whether you are religious or nonreligious, spiritual or nonspiritual. Your superconscious mind is the greatest power available to you, and properly directed, it can enable you to achieve any goal and reach any destination that you can set for yourself, as long as your goal is clear. It is one of the most important secrets of success.

Your superconscious mind attracts into your life people, ideas, and resources in harmony with your dominant thoughts. It brings you everything you need to succeed.

You can tap into your superconscious mind, like a supercomputer, at any time for ideas, solutions, guidance, and assistance. It becomes more powerful and grows in capability the more you use and believe in it. When you start to tap into your superconscious mind on a regular basis, it will begin to operate easily and automatically to solve your problems and achieve your goals.

It Requires Clear Commands

Your superconscious mind is activated by clear commands in the form of positive affirmations. These are the present-tense, positive, personal statements that you make from your conscious mind to your subconscious mind. Each time you make a positive affirmation or statement of your goal as if it were already realized, you activate your superconscious mind.

Emotionalized mental images, pictures, and visualizations also activate your superconscious mind. The greater clarity you have regarding the goals you desire and the more emotion with which you can visualize these goals, the faster your superconscious mind will bring them into your life.

It Works Automatically and Continuously

Your superconscious mind automatically and continuously solves every problem on the way to your goal, as long as your goal is clear. By writing out your goals clearly and specifically, you actually program them into your superconscious guidance system, where they then take on a life and a power of their own.

Whether you are awake, asleep, or busy with other activities, your superconscious mind works twenty-four hours a day. Once you have decided upon your goal, you can go about your daily life while your superconscious mind works on it, the same as you would do when you feed a question into a computer and let it run.

Your superconscious mind functions best with an attitude of calm, confident expectations. When you confidently believe and expect that you will achieve the exact goal or answer for you at exactly the right time, your superconscious mind will work quickly and efficiently.

This mind is always and instantly available to you to help you achieve any goal, solve any problem, or overcome any obstacle. It will solve your financial problems, lead you to your soul mate, and guide you to your heart's desire.

It Is Dedicated to Your Success and Happiness

Your superconscious mind is your devoted servant. It wants you to succeed and to succeed greatly. It wants you to be happy, healthy, and prosperous and enjoy a wonderful, satisfying life.

But your superconscious mind also knows that you need to learn certain lessons to be able to hold on to your success once you achieve it. This power will bring you these lessons one at a time, in sequence, like a good teacher instructing a student. Your job is to look into every setback or difficulty that you experience for the valuable lesson that it contains. Always ask yourself when things seem to go wrong, What can I learn from this experience?

Be Prepared to Take Immediate Action

Your superconscious mind will bring you exactly the answer you need at exactly the right time for you. But this answer will be "time dated." When you receive a superconscious answer, you must act on it immediately.

When you are working on a problem or goal and you get an impulse to make a phone call, buy a book, speak to a person, or take any particular action, move quickly. Don't delay. If you wait for twenty-four hours or even for a few minutes, it may be too late.

Your superconscious mind often speaks to you in the form of ideas. Some of the most successful people in history have achieved greatness by taking action on a single idea that shot into their mind like a bolt of lightning.

Activating Your Superconscious Mind

You can deliberately activate the powers of your superconscious mind in several ways. The first is simple. Take a sheet of paper and write down every detail of the problem you are facing. Sometimes the very act of writing out every detail of the problem or situation—how it occurred, what effect it's having, what you can do, and so on—triggers your superconscious mind into giving you the perfect solution.

Another way to activate your superconscious mind is to forget about the problem completely. Get so busy working on something else that you have no time at all to think about the problem. Then, at exactly the right time for you, the right answer will pop into your mind. But remember, when it does, you must take action immediately.

Throughout history, great men and women have tapped into their superconscious minds by meditation or what is called "mind calming." When you relax completely and let your mind go blank, very often a superconscious idea emerges.

My favorite way to activate the superconscious mind is the practice of *solitude*. To get the most out of a period of solitude, use this method. First, resolve to sit quietly by yourself for at least thirty minutes. It takes this long for your mind to relax completely.

Second, put away all distractions. Eliminate coffee, tea, reading materials, or anything else that might cause your attention to wander. This is called "going into the silence." When you sit quietly all by yourself, with no sound or distraction, and just let your mind go calm and clear, something wonderful happens. Writers often say that in a period of solitude, they were "touched by the muse."

Third, make no effort to think about your problem or goal at all. Let your mind relax completely. Don't try to think about anything. Simply sit quietly and let your mind wander gently around your life, thinking about nothing or everything. And at a certain moment, as you sit quietly, exactly the right answer that you need at this time will come in your mind.

Listening to gentle classical music can also activate your superconscious mind. Deep relaxation often triggers superconscious activity. Sometimes you will have a superconscious idea or answer while you are falling asleep or waking up. Keep a notepad by the side of your bed and quickly jot down any ideas or insights that occur to you so that you don't forget.

You can also activate your superconscious mind through physical activity—by walking, running, swimming, or engaging in any aerobic activity that increases your heart rate and triggers the release of endorphins and dopamine in your brain. These chemicals give you a feeling of happiness and euphoria and are often accompanied by superconscious inspirations. This is why many people have their best ideas in the shower after exercising.

When you learn about the superconscious and practice trusting in your superconscious mind, your potential will become unlimited. Your job is to tap into this mind and use it consciously, deliberately, and consistently. Have complete faith that it will work for you in exactly the right way at the right time, and it will.

The Superconscious Solution

Here are three ways that you can tell if you have received a superconscious solution:

1. A superconscious solution will be complete in every way. It will deal with every aspect of the problem or goal.

2. A superconscious solution will be a "blinding flash of the obvious." It will be simple, clear, and completely within your abilities to carry out. You will wonder why you had not thought of it before.

3. A superconscious idea or answer will come from your intuition. As a result, it will *feel* right. You will be relaxed and happy. Your stress and tension will disappear. You will be eager to implement it as soon as possible.

The Great Law

The Law of Superconscious Activity says, "Any thought, plan, goal, or idea held continuously in the conscious mind must be brought into reality by the superconscious mind."

This is an important definition. Your superconscious mind cannot work for you if you have a random series of unclear or contradictory goals or destinations. This is why the Bible says, "A double-minded man is unstable in all his ways."

The "single eye" is what enables you to unlock and unleash all your mental powers. Your ability to focus and concentrate is essential. Your superconscious mind goes to work for you when you decide upon your major definite purpose—the one goal that can have the greatest positive impact on your life—and you think about it continuously, holding it clearly in your conscious mind.

Your superconscious mind is activated when you step out in faith, when you take the first step, and the second and third steps, toward your goal. Most of all, your superconscious mind requires that you make continual course corrections, that you persist in the face of all adversity, and that you keep moving forward, no matter what happens.

When you combine all these activities, you will tap into the great powers of the universe to help you achieve any goal you truly desire.

CHAPTER TEN

Avoid Shortcuts and Other Mirages

Some men give up their designs when
they have almost reached the goal; while others,
on the contrary, obtain a victory by exerting,
at the last moment, more vigorous
efforts than ever before.

HERODOTUS

Perhaps the greatest enemy of personal success is explained by the Law of Least Resistance. Just as water flows downhill, most people continually seek the fastest and easiest way to get what they want, with very little thought or concern for the long-term consequences of their behavior. This natural tendency of people to take the easy way explains most underachievement and failure in adult life.

If you want to become physically fit, there is only one way. You must exercise two hundred minutes or more per week. For all-around fitness, you must engage in stretching exercises, strength-building exercises, and aerobic exercises. You must exercise your upper body and your lower body. And just like brushing your teeth or bathing, you have to do it throughout your life.

If you want to become mentally fit to maintain and increase your earning ability, you have to work out mentally as well. You have to read and study in your field each day. You have to keep current with what is going on in your industry. You have to listen to educational CDs rather than the radio in your car. You have to turn off the television and use your time to improve yourself personally and professionally. You have to resist the pull of the path of least resistance every single day.

Something for Nothing

One of the most powerful desires in humans is to get something for nothing or for as little as possible. It is tragic to see how many people are misled because of their hope or fantasy about somehow acquiring money quickly and easily. Tragically, the get-rich-quick and something-for-nothing people go from one easy-money scheme to another and ultimately end up with empty pockets and holes in their shoes.

Malcolm Forbes once wrote, "*If it sounds too good to be true, it probably is.*"

Be Prepared to Pay the Price

Nothing is as easy as it looks at the start. Nothing worthwhile is simple. Every great accomplishment is the result of hundreds and thousands of small efforts that nobody ever sees or appreciates. Every great fortune is the result of many years of hard work and experience; of sixty-, seventy- and eighty-hour weeks; of years without vacations and with countless setbacks, disappointments, unexpected turbulence, and headwinds.

Every so often, you read in the newspaper about people who start a high-tech company, or a dot-com like Google or YouTube, and become fabulously wealthy in a short period of time. But out of the twenty-six million businesses in America alone, these people represent a tiny fraction of 1 percent. They are written about in newspapers because they are so *rare*. Most enduring wealth is made up of serious money, accumulated slowly and carefully over a long period of time.

Practice the Four Cs of Flying

When you learn to fly a small plane, you are taught the "four Cs" to use if you get lost. These are "confess," "climb," "confirm," and "comply."

Face the Truth

The first C is "confess." As soon as you realize that you are lost, that you no longer know where you are flying by visual flight rules, you should contact the nearest tower and confess that you have a problem. In some situations, pilots of small planes, rather than admitting that they were lost, continued to fly in ever-widening circles until they ran out of gas and crashed.

Whenever you have a problem in your business or financial life, be prepared to confess this to someone who can help you. If you have a financial problem in your business, immediately tell your banker what is going on. Your banker has seen this type of situation hundreds of times and will be flexible with you. But bankers hate surprises. They don't want to learn too late that you cannot make your agreed-upon payments.

If your business is in trouble, don't be reluctant to find someone else in your same type of business and ask for advice. Most problems in business have been experienced countless times. Most of these problems have been solved countless times as well. Don't reinvent the wheel. Ask an experienced person for advice and counsel. Keep your ego out of the way.

Develop Proper Perspective

The second C is "climb." In an airplane, this means that you climb as high as you can so that you can see more of the landscape and maybe even find your bearings once more.

In your personal and business life, the equivalent of climbing is standing back from what you are doing and being completely honest with yourself regarding your situation and your problems. Act as your own consultant. Ask objective questions, such as the ones we have already discussed. Practice zero-based thinking. Refuse to get emotionally involved when things go sideways, as they always will.

Your ability to remain calm, cool, and confident will enable you to deal with any problem with a clear head and a focused mind.

Be Honest and Straightforward

The third C is "confirm." Tell the nearest radio tower who you are and what you can see. Answer the operator's questions honestly and objectively and to the best of your ability. Leave nothing out. The more information the operator has, the more likely it is that he or she will be able to help you get back on course.

In life, when you find yourself driven off course for whatever reason, immediately tell all the people who are involved. If you have a business problem, tell your staff exactly what it is and what you are doing to solve it. If you have a delivery or production problem, immediately call your customers and let them know what is going on. Don't be secretive. Don't keep vital information to yourself.

One of the most important truths in life and business is that everybody knows everything. There are no secrets. As soon as something happens, people begin talking about it, from one person to another. Rumors spread at incredible speed and get to the worst possible person who

can hear them. Tell people before they hear it from someone else.

When you were a child playing in the neighborhood
and you broke a neighbor's window, the rule was this:
"Beat the news home." You had to be sure that you got
home and told your father or mother what had happened
before the neighbor did. Parents don't like surprises
either.

In your work and personal life, you should also beat
the news home. Practice a "no surprises" policy. This insis-
tence on your part of being open, honest, and direct will
earn you a reputation for honesty and integrity. People
will trust you and believe you and be willing to support
you much more than if they find out the bad news on their
own. Remember, if you want people to trust you, the first
requirement is that you must be trustworthy.

Take the Advice of the Experts

The last *C* is "comply." You do whatever the tower operator tells you to do if you are lost in a small plane. You don't
argue, debate, or attempt to second-guess the expert. You
follow his or her instructions to the letter. The operator
has only one goal, and that is to help you to get safely back
to the ground. In your business and personal life, the situation is very much the same. When you ask for advice
from your bankers, lawyers, accountants, or business ad-
visors, you should be prepared to follow their advice

immediately to deal with your current situation. This doesn't mean that you should follow their advice blindly, but it does mean that you should act immediately to apply the advice if it makes sense to you and will help you solve your problem.

Be prepared to pay the full price of success in advance. Resist the natural temptation to get rich quick or get something for nothing. In the final analysis, the only way for you to achieve your goals is to make a valuable contribution, to add value of some kind. Never try to get rewards without working or to get anything that you are not entitled to by virtue of hard, hard work.

CHAPTER ELEVEN

Master Your Fears

**Courage is resistance to fear,
mastery of fear—not absence of fear.**

MARK TWAIN

Perhaps the greatest challenge that you will ever face in life is the conquest of fear and the development of courage. Fear is, and always has been, the greatest enemy of mankind.

When Franklin D. Roosevelt said, "The only thing we have to fear is fear itself," he was saying that the emotion of fear, rather than the reality of what we fear, is what causes us anxiety, stress, and unhappiness. When you develop the habit of courage and unshakable self-confidence, a whole new world of possibilities opens up for you. Just imagine—what would you dare to dream or be or do if you weren't afraid of anything in the whole world?

Develop the Habit of Courage

Fortunately, the habit of courage can be learned just as any other habit is learned, through repetition. We need to constantly face and overcome our fears to build up the kind of courage that will enable us to deal with the inevitable ups and downs of life unafraid. The starting point in overcoming fear and developing courage is to look at the factors that predispose us toward being afraid.

The root source of most fear is childhood conditioning, usually associated with *destructive criticism*. This causes us to develop two major types of fear. These are the fear of failure, which causes us to think "I can't, I can't, I can't," and the fear of rejection, which causes us to think "I have to, I have to, I have to."

When we are possessed by these fears, we become preoccupied with the possibility of losing our money, our time, or our emotional investment in a relationship. We become hypersensitive to the opinions and possible criticisms of others, sometimes to the point where we are afraid to do anything that anyone else might disapprove of.

Our fears can paralyze us, keeping us from taking constructive action in the direction of our dreams and goals. When we are in the grip of a fear, we hesitate and delay. We become indecisive. We procrastinate. We make excuses and find reasons to hold back. We feel frustrated, caught in the double bind of "I have to, but I can't" and "I can't, but I have to."

The More You Know, the Less You Fear

Fear is also caused by *ignorance*. When we have limited information, our doubts dominate us. We become tense and insecure about the outcome of our actions. Ignorance causes us to fear change, to fear the unknown, and to avoid trying anything new or different.

But the reverse is also true. The very act of gathering more and better information about a particular subject increases our courage and confidence in that area. You can see this in the parts of your life where you have no fear at all because you know what you are doing. You feel competent and completely capable of handling whatever happens.

Two other factors that contribute to fear are *illness* and *fatigue*. When you are tired or unwell, or when you are in poor physical condition, you are more predisposed to fear and doubt than when you are feeling healthy and full of energy.

Analyze Your Fears

Once you have identified the major factors that cause you to feel afraid, the next step is to objectively define and analyze your personal fears.

At the top of a clean sheet of paper, write, "What am I afraid of?" Remember, all intelligent people are afraid of something. It is normal and natural to be concerned about your physical, emotional, and financial safety and that of the people you care about. A courageous person is *not* a person who is unafraid. As Mark Twain said, "Courage is resistance to fear, mastery of fear—not absence of fear."

The issue is not whether you are afraid. We are all afraid. The only question is, How do you deal with the fear? A courageous person is someone who goes forward in spite of the fear. And here is an important point: when you confront your fears and move toward the source or cause of your fear, your fears diminish and your self-esteem and self-confidence increase. As Emerson wrote, "Do the thing you fear and the death of fear is certain."

The opposite is also true. When you avoid the thing you fear, your fears grow until they begin to control your life. And as your fears increase, your self-esteem, self-confidence, and self-respect diminish accordingly.

Make a List

Begin your list of fears by writing down everything, major and minor, that causes fear, stress, or anxiety. Think about the parts of your work or personal life where your fears might be holding you back or forcing you to stay in a job or relationship in which you are not happy. The most common fears, of course, are the fear of failure and the fear of rejection.

Some people, driven by the fear of failure, invest an enormous amount of energy justifying or covering up their mistakes. Others, saddled with the fear of rejection, are so obsessed with how they appear to others that they have no ability at all to take independent action. Until they are absolutely certain that someone else will approve, they cannot make a decision.

Once you have made a list of the fears that you think could be affecting your thinking and behavior, you should arrange your fears in order of importance. Which fear do you feel has the greatest impact on your behavior? Which holds you back more than any other? Which fear would be number two? What would be your third biggest fear?

Examine Your Fears Objectively

With regard to your predominant fear, write the answers to these three questions:

1. How does this fear hold me back in life?
2. How does this fear help me (or how has it helped me in the past)?
3. What would be my payoff for eliminating this fear?

When I went through this exercise myself some years ago, I concluded that my biggest fear was the *fear of poverty*. I was afraid of not having enough money, being broke, perhaps even being destitute. I knew that this fear had originated during my early childhood. My parents,

who had grown up during the Depression, had continually worried about money. This fear was reinforced when I
was broke at various times during my twenties. Even
though I could objectively assess the origins of this fear, it
still had a strong hold on me. Even when I had sufficient
money for all my needs, this fear was always there.

Ask the Key Questions

My answer to the first question, "How does this fear hold
me back in life?" was that it caused me to be anxious
about taking risks with money. It caused me to play it safe
with regard to employment. And it caused me to choose
security over opportunity.

My answer to the second question, "How does this
fear help me?" was that in order to escape the fear of
poverty, I worked longer and harder than most people. I
was more driven and determined. I took much more time
to inform myself on the various ways to make and invest
money. The fear of poverty was actually driving me
toward financial independence.

When I answered the third question, "What would be
my payoff for eliminating this fear?" I immediately saw
that I would be willing to take more risks. I would be
more aggressive in pursuing my financial goals. I would
start my own business. I would not be so tense and concerned about spending too much or having too little. I
would no longer be so concerned about the price of
everything.

By objectively analyzing my biggest fear in this way, I was able to begin the process of eliminating it. I was able to "turn fear into power" (as motivational speaker Tony Robbins is known for saying). And so can you.

Practice the Quality of Courage

You can begin the process of developing courage and eliminating fear by engaging in actions consistent with the habits of courage and self-confidence that you want to develop. Anything that you practice over and over eventually becomes a new habit.

The first and perhaps most important kind of courage for worldly success is the courage to begin, to launch, to step out in faith in the direction of your goal. This is the courage to try something new or different, to move out of your comfort zone, with no guarantee of success.

Robert Ronstadt, professor of entrepreneurship at Babson College for twelve years, conducted a follow-up study of his MBA students to find out how they had done later in life. To his surprise, less than 10 percent of his graduates had actually started their own businesses and become successful. The rest of them were working for other companies, still dreaming about becoming entrepreneurs one day. What could explain the difference between the two groups?

He could find only one quality that the successful entrepreneurs had in common: their willingness to actually start their own businesses rather than waiting. Ronstadt called this the "Corridor Principle." He found that as these individuals moved forward in their new businesses, as though proceeding down a corridor, doors of opportunity opened to them that they would not have seen if they had not been in forward motion.

It turned out that the graduates of his Entrepreneurship Program who had done nothing with what they had learned were still waiting for conditions to be *just right* before they began. They were unwilling to launch themselves down the corridor of uncertainty until they could somehow be assured that they would be successful— something that never happened.

The Future Belongs to the Risk Takers

The future belongs to the risk takers, not the security seekers. Life is perverse in the sense that the more you seek security, the less of it you have. But the more you seek opportunity, the more likely it is that you will achieve the security that you desire.

Whenever you feel fear or anxiety and you need to bolster your courage, switch your attention to your goals. Visualize your goals as realities. Imagine that you are already the person you want to be, enjoying the life you want to live.

Your conscious mind can hold only one thought at a time, a thought of desire or a thought of fear. When you discipline yourself to think and talk continually about your goals, you will minimize and cancel out your fears. As you focus on how you can achieve your goals, your confidence and courage will increase. You will take complete control over your emotions and your future.

The Law of Concentration says, "Whatever you dwell upon grows and increases in your life." The more you dwell on your goals, the more of them you will achieve.

The Development of Courage

The mastery of fear and the development of courage are essential prerequisites for a happy, successful life. When you commit yourself to developing the habit of courage, you will eventually reach the point where your fears no longer have any control over you. They will no longer play a major role in your decision making.

You will set big, challenging, exciting goals, and you will have the confidence of knowing that you can attain them. You will be able to face every situation with calmness and self-assurance. You will become unstoppable.

CHAPTER TWELVE

Persist Until You Succeed

Determine to become one of the best; sufficient money will almost automatically follow if you get to be one of the "best" in your chosen field, whatever it is.

DON G. MITCHELL

The most important single quality of success is self-discipline. Self-discipline is having the ability within yourself, based on your strength of character and willpower, to do what you should do when you should do it, whether you feel like it or not.

Character is the ability to follow through on a resolution after the enthusiasm with which the resolution was made has passed. It is not what you learn but whether or not you can dedicate and discipline yourself to pay the price, over and over, until you finally reach your goal. Self-discipline is required in each stage of your journey.

You need self-discipline to set your goals in the first place. You need self-discipline to make plans for their accomplishment. You need self-discipline to continually revise and upgrade your plans with new information. You need self-discipline to plan each day, set priorities on the use of your time, and concentrate on the most important task that you could be doing at any time.

You need self-discipline to invest in yourself every day, to develop personally and professionally, to learn what you need to learn so that you can achieve the goals that are possible for you. You need self-discipline to delay gratification, to save and invest your money so that you can achieve financial independence in the course of your working lifetime. You need self-discipline to keep your thoughts on your goals and dreams and keep them off your doubts and fears. You need self-discipline to respond positively and constructively in the face of setbacks and problems rather than becoming angry or depressed.

Persistence Is Self-Discipline in Action

Perhaps the greatest display of self-discipline is persisting when the going gets tough. Persistence is self-discipline in action. Persistence is the great measure of individual human character. Your persistence is, in fact, the true measure of your belief in yourself and your ability to succeed.

Each time that you persist in the face of adversity and disappointment, you build the habit of persistence. You build pride, power, and self-esteem into your character and your personality. You become stronger and more resolute. By persisting, you become more self-disciplined. You develop within yourself the iron quality of success, the one quality that will carry you forward and over any obstacle that life can throw in your path.

The legends of the great accomplishments of men and women throughout history are stories of the triumph of persistence. All great men and women have had to endure tremendous trials and tribulations before reaching the heights of success and achievement. The strength of character manifested in their unshakable resolve made them great.

Persistence Is the Hallmark of Success

Successful businesspeople and entrepreneurs seem to be possessed of indomitable willpower and unshakable persistence. Everyone in any field who succeeds greatly has to overcome tremendous adversity, often for many years, before he or she finally wins.

In 1890, America was in the grip of a terrible depression. Businesses failed all over the country, and people were laid off in the thousands. A businessman living in the Midwest lost his hotel in the midst of this depression and found himself with little money and lots of time on his hands. He decided to write a book to motivate and inspire others to persist and carry on in spite of the difficulties facing the nation.

His name was Orison Swett Marden. He took a room above a livery stable, and for an entire year he worked night and day writing a book by hand, which he entitled *Pushing to the Front*. This book told the stories of countless men and women who had persisted over and over again until they eventually succeeded.

At last, the book was done. Early in the evening, he finished the final page and, being both tired and hungry, went down the street to a small café for dinner. While he sat and ate, the livery stable caught fire. By the time he returned, his entire manuscript, more than 5,500 pages, had been destroyed by the flames.

Never Give Up

At first, he was overwhelmed with feelings of disappointment and discouragement. But then he realized that his entire book had been built around the importance of persisting in the face of adversity. Drawing on his inner resources, he went back to work and spent another year rewriting the book from the beginning. He refused to give up.

When the book was completed, he offered it to several publishers, but in the middle of the depression, which was then in its third year, no one was interested in a motivational book. He accepted the rejection calmly and decided to wait until the timing was better. He moved to Chicago and took another job.

One day, he mentioned his book to a friend who happened to know a publisher. The publisher read the manuscript and became very excited. He felt that this book was exactly what people should be reading in the middle of a depression—or at any other time. *Pushing to the Front* was subsequently published and became a runaway bestseller. It became a source of inspiration and encouragement for thousands of people.

Many top businesspeople and politicians said that *Pushing to the Front* was the book that brought America into the twentieth century. It had an enormous influence on the minds of decision makers throughout the country and became the greatest single classic in the history of personal development books to that time. It was read and digested by people such as Henry Ford, Thomas Edison, Harvey Firestone, and J. P. Morgan.

Get Going and Keep Going

Orison Swett Marden wrote in his book, "There are two essential requirements for success. The first is 'go-at-it-iveness,' and the second is 'stick-to-it-iveness.'" Referring to the quality of persistence, he wrote, "There is no failure for the man who realizes his power, who never knows when he is beaten; there is no failure for the determined endeavor, the unconquerable will. There is no failure for the man who gets up every time he falls, who rebounds like a rubber ball, who persists when everyone else gives up, who pushes on when everyone else turns back."

Persistence Is Your Greatest Asset

Perhaps your greatest asset is simply your ability to stay at a task longer than anyone else. B. C. Forbes, who founded *Forbes* magazine and built it into a major publication during the darkest days of the Depression, wrote, "History has demonstrated that the most notable winners usually encountered heartbreaking obstacles before they triumphed. They won because they refused to become discouraged by their defeats."

John D. Rockefeller, at one time the richest self-made man in the world, wrote, "I do not think there is any other quality so essential to success of any kind as the quality of perseverance. It overcomes almost everything, even nature."

Conrad Hilton, who started with a dream and a small hotel in Lubbock, Texas, and went on to build one of the most successful hotel corporations in the world, said, "Success seems to be connected with action. Successful men keep moving. They make mistakes, but they don't quit."

Disappointment Is Inevitable

Intelligent people, acting in their own best interests, do everything possible to minimize the number of problems and difficulties that they might experience in their day-to-day activities. Yet in spite of our best efforts, disappointments and adversity are normal and natural, unavoidable parts of life. It has been said that the only things that are inevitable are death and taxes. But experience proves that disappointment is also inevitable.

No matter how well you organize yourself and your activities, you will experience countless disappointments, setbacks, and obstacles over the course of your life. And the higher and more challenging the goals that you set for yourself, the more disappointments and difficulties you will experience.

This is the paradox: you cannot evolve and grow and reach your full potential except by facing adversity, dealing with it effectively, and learning from it. Most of the great lessons of life will come to you as the result of setbacks and temporary defeats, which you have done your utmost to avoid. Adversity therefore comes unbidden, unexpected, and unwanted, in spite of your best efforts. And yet without adversity, you cannot grow into the kind of person who is capable of achieving the great goals that are possible for you.

Adversity Is What Tests Us

Throughout history, great thinkers have reflected on this paradox and have concluded that adversity is the test that you must pass on the path to accomplishing anything worthwhile. Herodotus, the Greek philosopher, said,

"Adversity has the effect of drawing out strength and qualities of a man that would have lain dormant in its absence." The very best qualities of strength, courage, character, and persistence are brought out in you when you face your greatest challenges and when you respond to them positively and constructively.

Everyone faces difficulties every step of the way. The difference between high achievers and low achievers is simply that the high achievers utilize adversity to become stronger, while the low achievers allow difficulties and adversity to overwhelm them and leave them discouraged and dejected.

Success Is Always
One Step Beyond Failure

Your greatest successes almost invariably come one step beyond your greatest failures, when everything inside you says to quit. Men and women throughout history have been amazed to find that their great breakthroughs came about as a result of persisting in the face of disappointment and all evidence to the contrary. This final act of persistence, which is often called the "persistence test," seems to precede great achievements of all kinds.

H. Ross Perot, who started EDP Industries with $1,000 and built it into a fortune of almost $3 billion, is one of the most successful self-made entrepreneurs in American history. He said, "Most people give up just when they're about to achieve success. They quit on the one-yard line. They give up at the last minute of the game, one foot away from a winning touchdown."

The power to hold on in spite of everything, to endure—this is the winner's quality. Persistence is the ability to face defeat again and again without giving up—to push on in the face of great difficulty. There is a poem by an anonymous author that I think everyone should read and memorize and recite to himself or herself when tempted to quit or to stop trying. This poem is called "Don't Quit."

Don't Quit

When things go wrong, as they sometimes will,

When the road you're trudging seems all up hill,

When funds are low and the debts are high

And you want to smile, but you have to sigh,

When care is pressing you down a bit,

Rest, if you must, but don't you quit.

Life is queer with its twists and turns,

As every one of us sometimes learns,

And many a failure turns about

When he might have won had he stuck it out:

Don't give up though the pace seems slow—

You may succeed with another blow.

Success is failure turned inside out—

The silver tint of the clouds of doubt.

And you never can tell how close you are.

It may be near when it seems so far:

So stick to the fight when you're hardest hit—

It's when things seem worst that

you must not quit.

Success Is Not an Accident

Do not wait. The time will never be just right.
Start where you stand: work with
whatever tools you have at your command,
and the better tools will be found as you go along.

NAPOLEON HILL

The book of Ecclesiastes says, "Wisdom is the principal thing; therefore get wisdom; and with all thy getting get understanding." Throughout the ages, the acquisition of wisdom has been considered the highest human calling. The men and woman that we admire the most, living and dead, are those who attained high levels of wisdom over the course of their lives.

In our daily life, we seek out people who have the wisdom, coming from experience, to give us advice and guidance to help us avoid pitfalls and achieve our goals faster.

Aristotle wrote, "Wisdom is an equal measure of experience plus reflection." To develop wisdom for yourself, you must first have the experiences, and then you must reflect on them, extracting out of each experience every idea, insight, and kernel of knowledge that it contains.

The Person You Become

Most people have a dream, desire, and goal to make a lot of money and become financially independent. Almost everyone dreams of becoming a millionaire someday. And this goal is eminently achievable if you want it long enough and hard enough and you are willing to do the work necessary to achieve it.

But the most important part of becoming a millionaire, of achieving any goal or reaching any important destination, is not the goal itself. It is the person that you have to become to achieve that goal.

To achieve something that you have never achieved before, you must become someone that you have never been before. You must develop qualities and characteristics that you have never had before. You must learn talents and skills that you have never learned before. To achieve great success, you must become a great person. To become truly successful, however you define it, you must become a successful person in your own heart and mind.

Character Is Everything

When we see or talk with people we admire or when we hear or think about them, we seldom consider them in terms of material accomplishments. Instead, the men and women who stand out in our thinking are those who have become exceptional as a result of the experiences that they had, the things that they accomplished, and the character that they developed.

Your great goal in life is to fulfill your complete potential and become everything you are capable of becoming. Your goal is to become an exceptional person, possessed of character, competence, and wisdom. Your responsibility to yourself is to do something wonderful with your life and make a real difference in the world. This is the real secret of success.

True success in any area is usually the result of hundreds and maybe thousands of small and large things that you do or fail to do. There is no "key to success" or "secret." As the writer Og Mandino once told me, "*The great secret of success is that there are no secrets. There are merely universal ideas and principles that have been discovered and rediscovered over and over again.*"

The three most important steps, discovered and rediscovered by virtually every successful person, are these:

1. Decide exactly what you want, write it down, and make a plan to achieve it. Decide upon your destination.

2. Take action. Launch toward your goal. Step out in faith. Take the first step with no guarantee of success. Take off on your journey.

3. Be prepared to make continual course corrections every hour and every day of your life as you fly toward your destination. Expect an inevitable, unavoidable, and unbroken series of problems, difficulties, reversals, setbacks, and crises every day and week of your life. Since you cannot avoid them, your aim must be to respond to them effectively.

Make a decision right now to set your goal, take off, and make continual course corrections until you achieve all that is possible for you.

INDEX

Learning Resources of
Brian Tracy International

Brian Tracy — Speaker, Author, Consultant

Brian Tracy is one of the top business and personal success speakers in the world today. He has given more than five thousand talks and seminars for more than one thousand companies, including many of the world's largest.

He gives fast-moving, entertaining, high-content speeches and seminars to 250,000 people each year, speaking in forty-six countries on six continents.

His hard-hitting talks on leadership, sales, management and personal success bring about immediate and long-lasting change. Many of his graduates have gone on to great success and fortune after a single talk.

Brian has written forty-five books and produced more than 350 audio and video learning programs. His books and courses have been translated into thirty-six languages and are used in fifty-two countries. He is the top audio author in the world today.

Brian is available for talks and seminars worldwide. He carefully crafts and tailors each talk for your unique audience, using your industry and examples throughout.

Brian offers talks and seminars on the following subjects:

1. High Performance Selling
2. Leadership for the Twenty-first Century
3. Performing at Your Best
4. Superior Sales Management

To book Brian to speak for your company or group, please phone (858) 481-2977, extension 17, or e-mail VRisling@brian tracy.com.

Brian Tracy University of Sales and Entrepreneurship

To earn more, you must learn more! Now you can learn practical, proven strategies to attract more customers, make more sales, and increase your profits.

Brian Tracy University offers a complete series of practical, proven programs that have been applied successfully by more than 1,000,000 students in forty-six countries, based on work with more than one thousand companies.

Choose from four colleges of study:

1. **College of Sales and Sales Management**
   In this thirty-part home-study program, learn how to double and triple your sales; leads to a Certified Sales Professional designation.

2. **College of Entrepreneurship and Business Success**
   Learn the tools and techniques you need to build a highly profitable, fast-growth business; leads to a Master of Business Excellence certification.

3. **College of Management and Leadership**
   In this thirty-part High Performance Leadership program, learn how to recruit, hire, manage, motivate, and build a top team of excellent people; leads to a Master of Management certificate.

4. **College of Personal Performance**
   Learn how to set and achieve goals, set priorities, build your self-esteem and self-confidence, solve problems, and make better decisions; leads to a Master of Personal Excellence certification.

(continued)

In one hour per week, with video and audio programs, CDs, DVDs, books, and exercises, you can become one of the most skilled and highly paid people in your field. You will learn how to increase your income and improve your profitability immediately.

Visit http://Briantracyu.com today and take a free assessment to discover your strengths and weaknesses and learn how to achieve personal excellence in everything you do.

Brian Tracy University
462 Stevens Avenue, Suite 202
Solana Beach, CA 92075
(866) 505-8345
http://Briantracyu.com

ABOUT THE AUTHOR

Brian Tracy is one of America's top business speakers, a bestselling author, and one of the leading consultants and trainers on personal and professional development in the world today. He addresses 250,000 people each year on subjects ranging from personal success and leadership to managerial effectiveness, creativity, and sales. He has written more than thirty books and has produced more than three hundred audio and video learning programs. Much of Brian's work has been translated into other languages and is being used in fifty-two countries. He is co-author, with Campbell Fraser, of the Advanced Coaching and Mentoring Program and the Coaching Excellence Program.

Brian has consulted with more than one thousand companies—IBM, McDonnell Douglas, and the Million Dollar Round Table among them—and has trained more than 2,000,000 people personally. His ideas are proven, practical, and fast acting. His readers, seminar participants, and coaching clients learn a series of techniques and strategies that they can use immediately to get better results in their lives and careers.

About Berrett-Koehler Publishers

Berrett-Koehler is an independent publisher dedicated to an ambitious mission: **Creating a World That Works for All**.

We believe that to truly create a better world, action is needed at all levels—individual, organizational, and societal. At the individual level, our publications help people align their lives with their values and with their aspirations for a better world. At the organizational level, our publications promote progressive leadership and management practices, socially responsible approaches to business, and humane and effective organizations. At the societal level, our publications advance social and economic justice, shared prosperity, sustainability, and new solutions to national and global issues.

A major theme of our publications is "Opening Up New Space." They challenge conventional thinking, introduce new ideas, and foster positive change. Their common quest is changing the underlying beliefs, mindsets, institutions, and structures that keep generating the same cycles of problems, no matter who our leaders are or what improvement programs we adopt.

We strive to practice what we preach—to operate our publishing company in line with the ideas in our books. At the core of our approach is stewardship, which we define as a deep sense of responsibility to administer the company for the benefit of all of our "stakeholder" groups: authors, customers, employees, investors, service providers, and the communities and environment around us.

We are grateful to the thousands of readers, authors, and other friends of the company who consider themselves to be part of the "BK Community." We hope that you, too, will join us in our mission.

Be Connected

Visit Our Website

Go to www.bkconnection.com to read exclusive previews and excerpts of new books, find detailed information on all Berrett-Koehler titles and authors, browse subject-area libraries of books, and get special discounts.

Subscribe to Our Free E-Newsletter

Be the first to hear about new publications, special discount offers, exclusive articles, news about bestsellers, and more! Get on the list for our free e-newsletter by going to www.bk connection.com.

Get Quantity Discounts

Berrett-Koehler books are available at quantity discounts for orders of ten or more copies. Please call us toll-free at (800) 929-2929 or email us at bkp.orders@aidcvt.com.

Host a Reading Group

For tips on how to form and carry on a book reading group in your workplace or community, see our website at www.bk connection.com.

Join the BK Community

Thousands of readers of our books have become part of the "BK Community" by participating in events featuring our authors, reviewing draft manuscripts of forthcoming books, spreading the word about their favorite books, and supporting our publishing program in other ways. If you would like to join the BK Community, please contact us at bkcommunity@ bkpub.com.